TRUE STORIES OF
PIRATES

This edition first published in 2015 by Usborne Publishing Ltd,
Usborne House, 83-85 Saffron Hill,
London EC1N 8RT, England.
www.usborne.com

A catalogue record for this title is available
from the British Library.

JFMAMJJASON /14
ISBN 9781409593492   01880/5
Printed in Chatham, Kent, UK

USBORNE

TRUE STORIES OF
PIRATES

LUCY LETHBRIDGE

Contents

The Golden Age of Piracy

For as long as there has been trade shipped between nations, there have been pirates in every sea and ocean in the world. In the Mediterranean, the pirates were known as corsairs, and came mainly from the region of North Africa that Europeans used to call the Barbary Coast. The corsairs ruled the waves for 300 years, from the 15th century to the 18th century. They sailed in rowing galleys that were so light and easily handled that they were known as "skimmers" of the sea. A corsair galley was so silent that it could creep up on the flanks of a ship unawares, making only the faintest splashing sound.

But the most intense period of pirate activity was the thirty years between 1690 and 1720, which is sometimes called the Golden Age of Piracy. This was the time when trade was thriving between the European colonies in America and the Caribbean and the ports of Europe. In India, the British East India Company had established trade routes all over the East and Middle East. Merchant ships made long journeys across the world's oceans carrying silk, gold, silver, porcelain and other precious goods. It was a profitable time to be a pirate.

But the line between piracy and "legal" war-profiteering was often blurred. Governments were delighted to employ pirates to attack their enemies – but they tried to disguise the fact by calling them privateers instead. There were rich rewards to be had by plundering ships – whether on behalf of the King or simply for your own private gain. As Bartholomew Roberts, the most successful of all pirates of the Golden Age, said of the pirate's career: "It is a short life but a merry one."

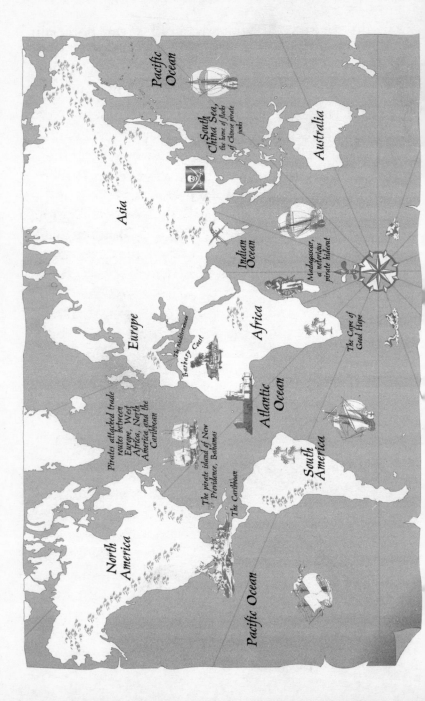

Pacific Ocean

South China Sea, the home of fleets of Chinese pirate junks

Australia

Asia

Indian Ocean

Madagascar, a notorious pirate hideout

Europe

The Mediterranean

Barbary Coast

Africa

The Cape of Good Hope

Atlantic Ocean

Pirates attacked trade routes between Europe, West Africa, North America, and the Caribbean

The pirate island of New Providence, Bahamas

The Caribbean

South America

North America

Pacific Ocean

The Capture of the Bird Galley

Early in the morning of 1719, the docks at Bristol, in the west of England, were already bustling with people. Under the fresh summer sunshine, there were sailors climbing riggings, swinging from ropes over the enormous beached hull of a ship they were coating with fresh tar. A line of men passed barrels, crates and bales into the hold of a ship due to leave for the Indies that day. Merchants, traders and, especially, slavers, inspected their cargoes, sniffed their wares or maybe pulled open the mouth of a manacled slave to check for healthy teeth. No one more than glanced up as a battered ship, the *Bristol Snow*, creaked slowly into dock.

Many such ships entered the port at Bristol every day: the city was the most important port in England for the slave trade. What could be special about yet another trader returning home from months at sea? But it was not long before word went around the city's taverns that William Snelgrave, the captain of the *Bristol Snow*, had an extraordinary story to tell. Snelgrave and his crew had spent over a month living with a notorious band of pirates. Few had ever survived such an ordeal and Snelgrave's account soon became the basis of a popular book - Daniel Defoe's *A General History of the Robberies and Murders of the Most Notorious Pirates*. It unlocked some of the secrets of the pirate world, a life of cruelty and violence inspired by the lure of riches and freedom - however short-lived.

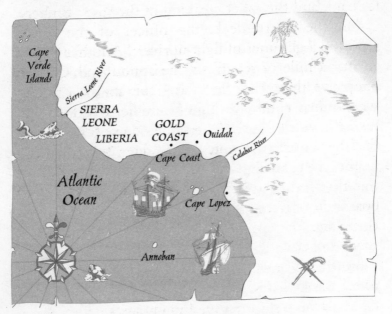

A map of the coast of West Africa

In the early spring of that year, Snelgrave had been captain of a slave ship named the *Bird Galley*, which had sailed slowly up the coast of West Africa, around the myriad tiny inlets that indent the coastline. The crew looked forward to returning home. It had been a long, hot voyage and they were tired of swatting mosquitoes and eating nothing but chewy dried beef and dry, hard biscuits. On April Fool's Day, the ship entered the mouth of the Sierra Leone River and dropped anchor for the night. The tropical night fell quickly and by seven o' clock that evening, the great river was shrouded in darkness. Nothing moved. There was no sound but the lapping of waves on the far bank and the quiet creaking of the ship's timbers.

On the quarterdeck, the officer of the watch reported a glimmer of light upriver: "Another ship at anchor a mile or so off, sir," he announced. Captain Snelgrave thought little of it – this stretch of coast was popular with slave ships – and he went below to his cabin to eat his supper. He could not have known that there were two more ships hidden behind a bend in the river. Snelgrave had barely lifted his glass of claret before the watch reported the sound of a small boat approaching the *Bird Galley*. Up on deck, they could hear the unmistakeable soft, rhythmic splash of rowing oars.

Immediately Captain Snelgrave ordered his first mate, Simon Jones, to send 20 men up onto the quarterdeck with firearms and cutlasses.

His second mate hailed the boat: "Ahoy there. Where you from?"

Through the hot night came an English voice. "Ahoy there. We're from a Barbados ship, from America."

This was followed instantly by a volley of small arms' fire. Captain Snelgrave felt his heart tighten: he knew for certain what kind of visitors these were.

"Fire!" he shouted to his men. "For God's sake, fire!"

But he was answered only by silence. Terrified, he demanded to know why none of the crew had taken up arms.

The reply came from below decks: "We can't find our firearms, sir. The chest where they're stored has disappeared."

Then another voice cut across him angrily: "You mean someone on board this ship has hidden it!"

Captain Snelgrave had no time to wonder at the identity of the saboteur. By now the strange boat had drawn alongside the ship and he could make out the dark shapes of men clambering over the ship's sides, hauling themselves over by ropes swung onto the decks and fastened with hooks. They swarmed like insects over the top. The first invader was a great brute of a fellow, a pistol strapped to his belt. Horrified, Captain Snelgrave realized that there was nothing they could do. The *Bird Galley* was entirely helpless.

The pirates threw a grenade through the trap door into the cramped quarters where the crew was cowering. Through the acrid smoke, the men emerged coughing and spluttering onto the deck. Immediately they raised their hands in surrender. In the chaos, the leader of the marauders, the pirate quartermaster, demanded to know who the captain was. Snelgrave was no coward.

He answered: "I have been the captain till now." The pirates stopped for a minute and made a rough circle around him, many of them grinning in anticipation of some sport. Then the quartermaster walked slowly over to Snelgrave and pushed his pistol against him.

"Why, I heard you, sir," he said close against Snelgrave's face. "You sir - you gave the order to fire and we don't like that, sir. It's not polite and to that we don't take kindly. Rules aboard our ship, sir, is that if you ain't polite, then you pay the penalty. Manners is manners."

"It is my duty to defend my ship," replied the terrified Snelgrave. The pirate made no response but pressed the muzzle of his gun into the captain's chest and pulled the trigger.

Later Snelgrave was to look back and wonder how he had been able to act so quickly. In a miraculous moment of quick thinking, he pushed the gun aside just as it went off and the bullet whistled past him, grazing his side bloodily but not fatally. Enraged, the pirate then brought his gun down with a loud crack on Snelgrave's head, knocking him to his knees.

He was dazed, but recovered himself and ran up the stairs and on to the quarterdeck. There in the smoke and shouting of the invaders, he met the pirate boatswain who raised his enormous broadsword and swung it at Snelgrave's head. The captain ducked and the sword fell on to the wooden planks of the deck, where it gouged a huge hole and shattered on impact. The boatswain swore loudly and began to hit Snelgrave - now too weak to fight back - over the head with the butt of his pistol. The crew, who watched in terror, pleaded with the boatswain to spare Snelgrave's life.

The boatswain paused. The pirates, who had enjoyed an easy victory over *Bird Galley*, were inclined to look mercifully on their captive Snelgrave, provided the ordinary seamen had no complaint against him.

Meanwhile, further up the river, those pirates remaining on their mother ship had seen candles and lanterns blazing peaceably on the *Bird Galley* and concluded that their fellows had been murdered by the seamen. They opened fire on the vessel while a bewildered Snelgrave yelled above the din: "Tell them we are taken peacefully!"

The pirate quartermaster shouted over the water that the *Bird Galley* was theirs and it was loaded with booty and strong drink. To the relief of Snelgrave and his men, the firing stopped immediately.

Not long afterwards, a small boat drew up alongside the ship. A short, stocky man climbed aboard wearing a tattered, once fine, velvet coat, its sleeves ragged with old lace. This was the pirates' captain, Thomas Cocklyn. He was a notorious pirate and Snelgrave had heard stories of his exploits around the African coast. He made Snelgrave a courteous bow.

"I'm sorry you have met with ill usage," he told him, "but 'tis the fortune of war sometimes."

Then he ordered the pirates to strip the *Bird*

Galley for food. The lives of pirates veered between feast and famine and the crew of the flotilla of ships which had captured the slaving vessel had been hiding in the river for weeks. The occasional fish or, if they were lucky, a pig shot on the riverbank, was not enough to feed three ships full of hungry men. The pirates were starving.

They appeared to have no interest in storing food for the future, but ate everything on board in one sitting. Cocklyn ordered every live animal on the ship to be killed immediately – geese, turkeys, chickens and ducks, as well as pigs and a huge pregnant sow. Snelgrave and his men were horrified to see that they didn't prepare the animals first. They simply ripped their guts out and singed the feathers of the fowl before throwing them all in a huge boiling cauldron – bristles, hooves, trotters and claws and all.

There were three pirate captains in charge of the flotilla: Howell Davies, Thomas Cocklyn and Oliver la Buze, known as "the Buzzard". Captain Cocklyn seemed to have taken a liking to Captain Snelgrave. He could see that he was respected by his men and this was a quality admired by pirates above all.

"All pirates are as one body," Cocklyn told his prisoner and fellow captain, "a kind of democracy. We don't set one man above another on a pirate ship but we cast votes for our captain and if he don't please us we vote him out again." Cocklyn decided to take the *Bird Galley* to be the pirates' raiding vessel: it was small and agile, useful for swift, silent movement in shallow water.

Snelgrave was surprised that the pirates had let him live. He had heard reports of their hideous barbarity to their prisoners. But for the next month he was left alone, able to observe the life and activities of the pirates in detail. Ten of his crew left him immediately to join the pirate gang. The group included first mate, Simon Jones. When Snelgrave tackled him about it, accusing him of disloyalty to his former shipmates, Jones looked amazed.

"Why, Captain Snelgrave - in my position, would you do anything else?" he retorted. "What life does a seaman have on a pitiful wage with nothing but hardship and stale rations to look forward to? I've a miserable marriage back at home and nothing to return to. I've been away so long I hardly now love or even recognize my wife. I always planned that if we were taken by pirates, I would do nothing to prevent their victory and would join them as soon as I was able to. That's why I hid the firearms' chest when I saw their boat coming towards us."

"But you risk your neck if you're caught," replied the captain. "You've seen the gibbets in big ports where the bodies of pirates swing as a warning to any who might be tempted to join them."

"It may be a short life but, while it lasts, I'll have gold in my pocket and I won't be working to fill the pockets of rich merchants and politicians back in England. And I'll have as much grog as I can drink."

Over the next two weeks, the crews of all three pirate vessels plundered the *Bird Galley*, draining it of all its valuables in an orgy of eating and drinking. Snelgrave was particularly shocked by the pirates' foul language.

"Execrable oaths and blasphemies … in hell itself I thought there could be no worse," he commented.

He could only stand and watch aghast as the pirates broke into the hold and hoisted upon deck dozens of half-hogsheads of claret and French brandy. They didn't even bother to remove the corks off the bottles. They just sliced the necks off with a cutlass. Later they swabbed the decks with whatever was left over. Some of the pirates played football with Snelgrave's gold watch; another drunk stole his hat and wig. Anything they couldn't find a use for was thrown overboard or set alight with a piece of flaming rag dipped in tar. Snelgrave was forced to look on helplessly as the pirates gleefully threw his precious possessions into the water.

These riotous antics lasted for two days, unchecked by their captains. Pirate captains were leaders in battle only. When it came to the spoils, everyone was equal in a pirate ship and there were no special privileges for the captain. This astounded Snelgrave, who was accustomed to Royal Navy rules, by which the captain enjoyed his own cabin and slept in a bed with linen sheets, while his crew made do with hammocks slung between damp timbers. He ate meat prepared specially for him in the galley, while the crew had thin soup or dry biscuits. Cocklyn and the other captains had taken three of Snelgrave's finest coats, which they decided to wear on a jaunt ashore to meet the local ladies. Cocklyn had helped himself to a silver embroidered one which, since he was so short, trailed along the floor behind him. The ordinary pirates were furious that their captains should have broken pirate law by taking the coats without permission from the quartermaster. So, when Davis, Cocklyn and La Buze returned aboard, the coats were stripped from their backs and put into the common chest to be sold to the highest bidder.

Acts of casual cruelty combined bewilderingly with loyalty and kindness. One of the pirates, a man named Williams, accused Snelgrave of encouraging the captains to take his coats. He held his knife under Snelgrave's chin and threatened to kill him. But another pirate nudged the quaking Snelgrave in the ribs.

"He always talks like that. But if you call him 'captain' he'll calm down." Snelgrave took his advice, addressed Williams as "captain" and in doing so found himself an unlikely friend and protector. That evening, Williams proudly presented him with a keg of wine. He pulled the cork out with his two black teeth and handed it to Snelgrove with a comradely grin.

Finally, after a month of captivity, when the liquor barrels had been drunk dry and the food had run out, the pirate captains and crew held a council to decide on the fate of Snelgrave and his remaining men. Each pirate spoke up in turn and argued the case for or against the killing of their captives.

Snelgrave was a fine captain, one pirate claimed, but another pointed out that he might give evidence against them in court if they were ever captured. In the end, however, they decided to let him go. And they gave him a fighting chance of getting back to England, by letting him have the *Bristol Snow*, one of the ships they had won in battle. The pirates even presented him with treasure worth many thousands of pounds, and held a farewell party to see the *Bristol Snow* on its way.

During the festivities, a fire broke out when someone put a candle too near to a cask of rum and the cask exploded. With 30,000 pounds of gunpowder on board, it might have ended in disaster, but those pirates sober enough to think straight huddled at one end of the ship while the others made for the boats. Sixteen men, most of them from Snelgrave's remaining crew, battled the fire until it was finally put out.

That night, Snelgrave boarded the *Bristol Snow* to begin the slow voyage back to England. The journey took several weeks. The captain and his crew (numbering only about 15 men) were jumpy and nervous whenever the ship anchored in sheltered inlets or when they saw the shape of an unknown vessel looming on the horizon. So they were all enormously relieved when they saw the familiar cool rainclouds of the Bristol Channel and the ship finally entered port.

In the warm taverns on the dockside, Snelgrave and his men told the story of their capture over welcome pints of ale. Stories about pirates were common in those days, but many of them were exaggerated – or just based on popular myths. The crew of the *Bird Galley* kept their listeners enthralled. Most of the local people had known someone who had been a victim of pirates – but, unlike the men of the *Bird Galley*, none of the others had survived to tell their tale.

Long Ben, the Arch-Pirate

In 1720, on the stage of the Theatre Royal in London's Drury Lane, a menacing figure strutted across the boards. His face, painted vivid red and grimacing and leering, was horrible in the dim candlelight. He was wearing a faded velvet tail coat and on his head was a tattered tricorn hat; behind him waved a familiar flag decorated with the skull and crossbones. The audience roared with laughter and delight. *The Successful Pirate* had been running at the theatre for several weeks and was a sell-out success - not surprisingly, when its starring character was the most famous, and elusive, pirate of the day.

Henry Every sometimes called himself Avery and was known to his pirate crews as "Long Ben". But to the people of England where he had become a legend, he was simply the "arch-pirate". News of Every's spectacular coup in overcoming a heavily-armed Mogul ship, and making off with Indian treasures worth millions, had filtered back to his homeland and made him a hero among the English poor. Legends of the arch-pirate abounded. Had he really died a squire in Devon? Had he offered to pay off the national debt in return for a pardon? Had he married a Mogul princess and taken her to live with him in the pirates' fiefdom of Madagascar? The writer Daniel Defoe wrote that his exploits had "raised him to the dignity of a king." On the streets of London, the ballad-sellers sold songs about Every's courage in plundering the ships of the ruler of India, the Great Mogul himself:

"Come, all you brave boys whose courage is bold.
Will you venture with me? I'll glut you with gold.
Make haste unto Corunna; a ship you will find
That's called the Fancy will pleasure your mind."

Admired as a rebel by the ordinary people, Henry Every was hated by the English authorities. The government had promised the Great Mogul to drive the pirate emperor of the Eastern Seas out of India's territory forever. They put a price of £500 on his head and the East India Company added to that another £1,000. In addition, the government declared him exempt from the various Acts of Grace that were occasionally passed by parliament to pardon pirates. But Henry Every was never captured. The most celebrated pirate of his age died in his own bed – though nobody ever knew where that was.

In 1695, the *Gang-I-Sawai* was by far the greatest of the Great Mogul's formidable fleet of ships. It was vast, carrying 62 guns, 400 to 500 musketeers and

600 passengers. It was thought to be so impregnable that it needed only one armed ship to escort it: the much smaller *Fateh Mohammed*. In August of 1695, the *Fateh Mohammed* lagged behind a great convoy of 25 treasure ships moving down the Red Sea to the Indian Ocean, heading for Surat in India. Among those on board the ship were Muslim officials of the Mogul's court who were returning from a pilgrimage to Mecca in Arabia. The ship was also carrying a cargo of gold and silver pieces worth half a million pounds. Surat was still an eight day sail away.

Map of the Eastern Seas, where Long Ben carried out his raids

As the *Gang-I-Sawai* and her convoy approached the mouth of the Red Sea, a fleet of pirate ships was waiting for them. Henry Every, its supreme commander, was on the quarterdeck of his ship, the *Fancy*. The *Fateh Mohammed* was the pirates' first target. As soon as the ship came into view, it was quickly flanked by two pirate schooners. Caught unawares, her sailors put up little fight when they were boarded by the pirates. Every's men found £50,000 in gold and silver aboard.

The pirates then pursued the *Gang-I-Sawai* into the Indian Ocean. Despite a formidable array of guns, the Indian ship proved a surprisingly easy conquest. One of the guns misfired, which caused confusion among her crew and gave the pirates time to clamber up its vast sides and get quickly on board. The captain, Ibrahim Khan, rushed downstairs to lock up some of the women they had been transporting to India from Turkey to be concubines.

After two hours of bloody fighting with cutlasses and daggers, the ship fell finally into the hands of the pirates. They tore open the carefully-stowed chests and caskets they found in the hold, pulling out gold, silver and jewels: examples of the great wealth of the Indian princes. This included a magnificent saddle, made in Arabia, set with enormous, glowing rubies. It was to be a gift to the Great Mogul from the returning pilgrims.

It was a barbaric orgy of violence and looting. The sailors of the *Gang-I-Sawai* tried to pretend the female passengers were men by dressing them in turbans. But Every's hardened crew took no notice. Some of the women even threw themselves overboard or attempted to stab themselves with daggers to prevent themselves from being captured. Among them was the aristocratic wife of an "umbraw"– a Mogul court official, who was returning from Mecca. Perhaps it was her presence on the ship that led to the story of Henry Every's Mogul princess bride. The horrible truth of the pillaging of the *Gang-I-Sawai* was not heroic at all: few of the women on board the ship survived. They were either thrown into the sea or put ashore, disgraced and humiliated, at the island of Réunion where the ship finally docked.

So who was Henry Every, the arch-pirate of legend and the sickeningly violent looter of the *Gang-I-Sawai?* One contemporary account described him like this:

He was middle-sized, inclinable to be fat and of a jolly complexion, but insolent and uneasy at times, and always unforgiving if at any time imposed upon. His manner of living was imprinted on his face, and his profession might easily be told from it. His knowledge of his profession was great, being founded on a strong natural judgement, and sufficient experience advanced by incessant application to mathematics. He still had many principles of morality which many subjects of the King have experienced.

Henry Every's early life is unclear. What we do know is that he came to piracy relatively late in life. It is thought that he was born near Plymouth, in the west of England, in about 1653 - some said he was the son of a prosperous tavern keeper. He was by all acounts a clever boy and his family wanted him to be a scholar. But he went to sea when he was very young, aged only about 11, and became a cabin boy on a merchant vessel. There he became a particular friend of the captain and slept in a hammock in the captain's cabin.

In 1694, Every was in his early forties and working as the first mate of a ship sailing from Bristol, named *Charles II* after the English king. It had been chartered by the Spanish government to intercept French smugglers. The ship was well-armed, carrying 46 guns; it was just the right type of neat, versatile, fast-moving vessel that pirates like to use. Every and his fellow sailors fell into discussion when Captain Gibson was drunk, as he so often was.

"He's always sleeping after a night on the rum. It'll be easy," murmured one to the other.

Every started thinking. If they took the *Charles*, it meant giving up all thoughts of a quiet retirement; turning pirate meant being hunted down for the rest of your life. But he didn't have to think about it for long. He was weary of the low rations, the stingy pay and the dog's life of working as a sailor under a useless layabout like Captain Gibson.

"I'll do it," he said. The others nodded in agreement. Every was their choice as captain; he was popular with the men. His easy-going personality hid a flinty ruthlessness. He would be a decisive leader.

In the end, it was ridiculously easy. The *Charles* had put into the Spanish port of La Coruña, when Captain Gibson took his usual drop. (Daniel Defoe later reported that he was "mightily addicted to punch".) He was snoring loudly in his bunk, when the mutineers battened down the hatches, weighed the anchor and sailed the *Charles* out into the Atlantic. When the captain finally roused himself, he heard Every's menacing whisper in his ear.

"I am captain now, Mr. Gibson,"said the pirate softly, "and you'd be advised to take my orders from now on."

Captain Gibson refused to join the mutineers. He didn't have the stomach for a life of piracy. So he and five loyal companions were unceremoniously dumped into a ship's rowing boat and left to make their own way to shore.

As for Every and his men, they renamed the ship the *Fancy* and pulled up a new flag comprising four silver chevrons (diagonal lines) on a red background. Then they set off through the treacherously dangerous seas of the Cape of Good Hope to the island of Madagascar in the Indian Ocean. It was a notorious pirate hideout, its many small coastal inlets made a perfect hiding place for a fleet of pirate ships wanting to lie low. In some parts of the island, pirates ruled as kings. On the way to Madagascar, Every aimed to take advantage of the ships that ran across their path on the Eastern Seas. It was a fertile hunting ground, with Arab ships bearing gold and spices and, of course, the treasure-laden fleets of the Great Mogul himself. For first time pirates, they had an amazing run of success: they took three English ships in succession off the Cape Verde Islands. Then they rounded the Cape of Good Hope again, and took refuge on the island of Johanna, where they stripped off some of the heavy wooden body of the *Fancy* to make her a sleeker shape and capable of sailing faster.

While they were working in Johanna, a French pirate ship entered the inlet where they were hidden. It was weighed down with loot robbed from Moorish ships off the coast of North Africa. Every seized the ship with surprisingly little difficulty. Shortly afterwards, 40 of the French pirates joined the crew of the *Fancy*. Every was now in charge of a fleet of ships – the *Fancy*, the French prize, and two of the English ships he had captured previously.

Just before he left Johanna, Every, who was arrogantly enjoying to the full his new life as a pirate high commander, wrote an open letter which he left with a native chief, to be given to the first English ship that put in to the island. It was addressed to:

All English commanders,

Let this satisfy that I was riding here at this instant in the ship Fancy, man of war, formerly the Charles of the Spanish Expedition who departed from La Coruña May 7, 1694, being then and now a ship of 46 guns, 150 men and bound to seek our fortunes. I have never as yet wronged any English or Dutch, or ever intend while I am commander. Wherefore as I commonly speak with all ships I desire whoever comes to the perusal of this to take this signal, that if you or any whom you may inform are desirous to know what we are at a distance, then make your ancient [ship's flag] up in a ball or bundle and hoist him at the mizen peak, the mizen being furled, I shall answer with the same, and never molest you, for my men are hungry, stout and resolute, and should they exceed my desire I cannot help myself. As yet an Englishman's friend.

At Johanna, February 18, 1695

Henry Every

As Long Ben Every had already taken three English ships as prizes, this sudden claim of patriotism hardly rang true. And the British government was certainly not tempted to act indulgently towards him because he was an Englishman. After all, when the *Gang-i-Sawai* was taken just a few months later, it was the English East India Company who had to foot the bill for the ship's Indian owners. In fact the entire trading operation of the Company was under threat simply because of the enormous sums they had to pay for losses on Indian ships attacked by English and American pirates. From now on, Every was top of the government's most-wanted list. After a few brief months of piracy, he and his men were so notorious that they would never safely walk the streets of a British city under their own names again.

But it was the capture of the *Gang-I-Sawai* that ensured Every's lasting fame. When the loot was divided among the crew of the *Fancy* and the rest of the fleet, the pirates got £1,000 each and a quantity of jewels. In today's money that might be worth nearly half a million pounds – more than three-quarters of a million dollars. But Every received the due that was given to all pirate captains: just two shares.

After the division of the plunder, Every's fleet split up. Every himself decided to take the *Fancy* to the Bahamas, despite the fact that many of the men wanted to go to Brazil, where they had heard tales of

Map of the Caribbean, where some of the pirates settled

rich pickings to be had from trading ships. More than 50 of them took their money and settled down to become prosperous, law-abiding merchants on the French island of Réunion in the Indian Ocean.

To fill the gaps in his workforce, Every took on board 90 African slaves. In April 1696, the *Fancy* set sail across the Atlantic to the Caribbean where, at the island of St. Thomas, they put some of their booty up for sale. The locals had never seen such a hoard of lovely things. Père Labat, a Jesuit priest working there, wrote later that, "a roll of muslin embroidered with gold could be obtained for only 20 sols and the rest of the cargo in proportion." No wonder pirates were popular in the Caribbean: they brought bags of money with them and luxuries on offer at low prices.

In the Bahamas, the Governor, Nicholas Trott, welcomed the pirates – although they first had to grease his palm with 20 pieces-of-eight and two pieces of gold each, besides ivory and other treasures. They were royally entertained at the Governor's table, but he was not permitted to pardon them; he did not have the authority. The *Fancy* had to move on, trying to buy pardons from the Governor of Jamaica and others, in exchange for a few luxury items from the *Gang-I-Sawai*.

Every's crew divided and scattered. Some of his men went to the Carolinas, and some to New England, on the coast of North America; others took the risk of discovery and stayed in the Caribbean.

Every himself changed his name to Benjamin Bridgeman and sailed for Ireland with 20 other men in a sloop named the *Seaflower*. They landed at the isolated, bleak coastal town of Dunfanaghy on the north coast. From this point, Long Ben vanished into the Irish mist.

The other men were not so cunning. Several of them were captured in the town of Westport, County Mayo, after offering the incredulous locals sackloads of gold and silver in exchange for old horses that weren't worth a tinker's sixpence. One man had carefully quilted his coat with gold doubloons. When he handed it in to a maid in a tavern, she was astonished at the weight and went off to tell the mayor of her suspicions. The man was arrested soon afterwards.

But Henry Every, the arch-pirate and scourge of the Eastern Seas, was never seen again. Daniel Defoe, who liked to embroider a good story, put it about that he had been cheated by the Bristol merchants on whom he'd tried to offload his ill-gotten gains and had died a pauper in Devon. But others claimed he had retired a wealthy man and lived like a squire in the West Country until the end of his days.

The Count of Ericeira's Diamonds

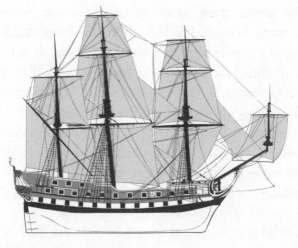

A Portuguese Indiaman, one of the sturdy ships that sailed between Europe and India in the 18th century

Dom Luis Carlos Ignacio Xavier de Meneses, the fifth Count of Ericeira, was among the most cultured men of the Portuguese aristocracy. For several years he had been Viceroy of the Portuguese colony of Goa, on the southwest coast of India. The Count was well-educated and elegant. He was also brave - and his courage was to be tested in his hair-raising encounter with pirates in April 1721.

The story began when the Count was returning home to Portugal from Goa after his post as viceroy had come to an end. During his time in India, the Count had amassed an impressive collection of the finest diamonds. He was hoping that the diamonds would restore his family fortunes; but there were also some gems destined for the King of Portugal.

The Count of Ericeira was a passenger on the *Nossa Senhora do Cabo*, a solidly-built Portuguese Indiaman, one of the sturdy, wide-bottomed ships that plied the trade routes between India and Europe. The *Cabo* was crammed with wonderful goods: Chinese silks, blue and white porcelain, tea, silver, gold, jars of spices and bales of embroidered textiles were stashed away in the ship's hold. But the most valuable thing on board was the Count's diamonds. There were so many of them that they were stored in ten sacks weighing nearly two pounds each.

For a pirate working the Indian Ocean, it would be the haul of a lifetime – beyond even their wildest dreams. The attack on the *Cabo* on April 26 1721 amounted to the most staggeringly lucrative coup in the history of piracy. It was an English pirate captain, John Taylor, in his ship *Cassandra*, accompanied by a French pirate, Oliver La Buze "the Buzzard" in the *Victory*, who had the good fortune to pull it off.

The *Cabo* had had her mast torn off in a storm near Mauritius and was sheltering for repairs in St. Denis, on the nearby island of Bourbon. As the *Cassandra* and the *Victory* nosed around the entrance to the port, they came face to face with the great bulk of the *Cabo*: out of action and mastless, she was a sitting duck.

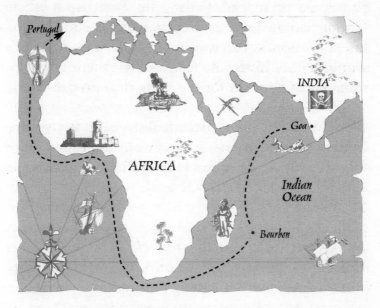

Map showing the Count of Ericeira's route

The Count, seeing the ships approach flying an English flag, ordered his men to salute them, as was customary. When they did not salute him in return but kept approaching at the same speed, he began to be suspicious. But it was too late. The ships had already come alongside the *Cabo* – one on either side of her vast wooden flanks, in a fatal pincer grip. Then they hauled down the English flags they'd been flying and raised instead the dreaded skull and crossbones pennants. The Count, with the crew and passengers of the *Cabo*, watched helplessly, then dived for cover, as the pirates fired a massive broadside into the huge East Indiaman.

Through the acrid smoke, they watched as 200

pirates clambered onto the ship from both sides, howling abuse to terrify their victims. Thirteen of the 130 inadequately-armed Portuguese sailors immediately defected to the enemy: they knew they were beaten. But the Count refused to give in. From the quarterdeck he took on the pirates with his sword. When the sword was finally broken in two, the Count fell into hand-to-hand combat, which only ceased when Captain Taylor ordered the pirates to stop. The battle had been lost.

Pirates admired courage in battle above all else and the Count had earned their respect. Instead of stealing his beautiful, now broken, sword, with its diamond encrusted hilt, they returned it to him.

Then they set to work pulling open the crates in the hold to inspect their loot. And what a loot it was! Out came spools of brightly woven silk, lovely decorated porcelain wrapped carefully in straw, the finest jewels, and ... diamonds! The pirates had never seen a such an incredible haul of diamonds like the Count of Ericeira's. It was a worth more than 100,000 times what a legitimate sailor could expect to earn in a year. At the great share-out, the prize amounted to 42 diamonds for every member of the pirate crew. One of them was given one large stone - reckoned to be the equivalent of the 42 - and, feeling himself to be short-changed, he took a hammer and smashed it into dozens of tiny pieces, wrongly believing that lots of small diamond chips would be more valuable than a single gem.

Although the pirates drew the line at sacrificing a single stone from the bags of diamonds, they wanted to show their respect for the Count by returning some of his personal belongings. But he proudly refused, saying he didn't wish to be singled out – he would never accept a privilege not accorded to the others. The pirates simply shrugged – what did they care? And the Count had to watch, horrified, as they casually ripped up his valuable oriental books and ancient manuscripts to serve as cartridge paper for their guns.

The pirates rightly guessed that a person as important and distinguished as the Count of Ericeira would be worth a ransom. They held him on board until the Governor of the island of Bourbon had given them a substantial sum in exchange for the Count's freedom. Then they decorated a special boat with pieces of the finest silk, roughly torn up into flags, and ceremoniously rowed him to the mainland. On board the *Cabo*, the rest of the pirates fired a viceregal 21-gun salute and shouted, "Vive le roi!"or "Long live the King!"

But when the Count returned home to Portugal, he found little sympathy for his plight. Quite the opposite in fact. The King and Queen of Portugal claimed that many of the diamonds had belonged to them all along and banished him from court for ten years as a punishment.

Into the Pirates' Lair

Map of the Caribbean, a haven for pirates in the 18th century

In 1718, in the colonies of the Bahamas, the inhabitants used to say you could smell the island of New Providence long before you set foot there. It was a sour stench, an unpleasant mixture of rum (or more probably rumfustian, a lethal combination of beer, gin and sherry mixed with spices), hot tar, human sweat and filth, rotting meat, mangy chickens and pigs, and steaming pots of salmagundi – made from turtles' flesh, pigs' trotters, onions, cabbage, hot peppers and everything else that could conceivably be edible.

But not many of the Bahamian colonists, trying to scratch a difficult living out of the rough soil of the islands, would have chosen to go to New Providence anyway. It was the pirates' island, and the port of Nassau, with its shallow, sheltered bay, was the perfect haven for them to hole up in with their ships. Too shallow for a Royal Navy man-of-war, its waters were exactly the right depth for the speedy little sloops the pirates preferred.

New Providence was where they went to count their money and to spend it on prostitutes, drink and gambling. It was also where they repaired their ships, protected by the lookout tower of the old fort there, where they stationed a continual watch. Order, of a kind, was kept by a rotation of men, their clothes smeared with tar as a protection against knife attacks.

The pirates changed the figureheads on stolen ships to escape identification and they careened their stolen vessels, coating them with a mixture of tar, tallow and chemicals, as a shield against the dreaded teredo worm. The worm was among the pirates' worst enemies. A blind, long, white invertebrate, like a hollow tube, the worm infests tropical waters and tunnels its way relentlessly through damp wood. The submerged hull of a wooden ship is a feeding frenzy of teredo worms. In the 17th and 18th centuries, the only protection a ship had against the teredo was this stinking ointment, which had to be applied three times a year.

The story goes that when an old pirate dies he goes to New Providence. It should have been a paradise, with its plentiful supply of turtles, lobster, conch, wild pigs and fresh water, but in fact it resembled a scene from hell. The worst villains among the pirates could be found holed up there, boozing, gambling and brawling.

Back in England, Captain Woodes Rogers had heard about New Providence Island and its fresh water, abundant vegetation and wild pigs. But he also knew it was a pirate colony with a terrible reputation. As the leading sea captain of his day, Rogers thought he could turn New Providence into a healthy settlement. Of course, it would be necessary to clear out the pirates first, but he had once been a successful privateer in the employ of the King, and had engaged in some "legal" pirate work himself in his time. He knew the pirates' tricks and dodges. Rogers came up with a plan to develop the Bahamas, to make them a base for English trade across the world. He would encourage people to come and live there, and make a living through farming and fishing. And, what is more, the pirates would be removed from their stinking den once and for all.

The British government was only too happy to listen to anyone who was prepared to take on the Caribbean pirates. By 1718, trade in the region had ground to a standstill. Ships could only leave Jamaica under armed naval escort.

"There is hardly one ship or vessel coming or

going out of this island that is not plundered," wrote the Governor of Jamaica. More than that, the navy itself had learned to profit from piracy. The deal was simple: pirates did not attack the naval convoys and in return the captains of the naval men-of-war did not attack the pirates. Convoys were good business: men of war could be hired for up to 12.5% of the value of a cargo. No wonder it was in the interests of naval convoy captains to keep piracy going.

This was the era of the terrible reign of Edward Teach, the pirate known as "Blackbeard" on account of his nightmarishly menacing long black beard – a beard he decorated with lighted candles, in order to terrify his victims more thoroughly. He was the most notorious of all pirates. From his lair in Oracoke Inlet on the coast of North Carolina, he was the dread of every sailor setting out across the Caribbean. The rewards for pirates in New Providence Island were not as great as for those who attacked in the Eastern Seas, but they had a lot less chance of getting caught.

It was in this atmosphere of fear that Rogers persuaded King George I to appoint him Governor of the Bahamas. His promise was to attack the very heart of the pirates' operations and in doing so to put a stop to their activities. Rogers managed to convince the King that he could turn a rabble of dangerous, drunken men into model farmers and a prosperous colony of well-behaved Christian citizens.

The plan was to offer the pirates a full pardon and the opportunity to settle down with a plot of land in the Bahamas, on the condition that they reformed their wicked ways. As many as 250 settler families, Rogers estimated, could live harmoniously on New Providence. In fact, he promised the King that they would soon all be God-fearing subjects of His Majesty. There was something in it for him too: Woodes Rogers himself would take a share of any profits that might be earned by the new colony.

The King agreed to the plan. Furthermore, the Secretary of War gave Rogers 100 foot soldiers to take with him to the Bahamas, and the Admiralty presented him with an escort of warships. He was also given stores, tools and materials – and he even had some evangelical religious tracts printed, which he aimed to distribute around the island in an attempt to steer the pirates from their evil ways. The government gave him a 21-year lease on the Bahamas. Rogers reckoned that would give him time enough to make the project work.

In London, during the winter of 1717, Rogers worked hard to get his expedition ready. In the spring of 1718, he set sail down the Thames in the *Delicia*, accompanied by two Royal Navy frigates and two smaller sloops. The new Governor was a battle-hardened veteran of spats with pirates, but even he didn't really know what to expect from the islands, or what kind of resistance the mob on New Providence would put up against him. But at least the Government had promised they would support him with troops as he needed them.

It took Rogers and his convoy three long months to get to Nassau, home of a thousand pirates. At first it all seemed deceptively easy: English colonists on nearby Harbour Island saw the fleet moored just outside the long spit of sand at the entrance to Nassau's sheltered bay. They rowed out to Rogers's ship to deliver the news that most of the pirates of Nassau were willing to surrender immediately. They were prepared to accept their pardons and even to become citizens of the new colony of the Bahamas.

But Rogers suspected that victory wasn't going to be that easy. In fact, the monstrous Blackbeard had decamped to his hideout on Oracoke Inlet, where he and his men were planning a final massive attack on shipping coming out of Jamaica. But there were other resisters among the pirates too. Most of them were led by Charles Vane, a seasoned pirate captain who intended to hold out against the forces of the King for as long as possible.

As the warships edged slowly past the sandy spit and towards Nassau, Vane gave them a glowing welcome, with bonfires that sent fountains of flame high into the night air, and great cracks from gunpowder grenades exploding around them. He had set alight a recently captured French ship and set her adrift into the still waters of the bay, where she listed towards the convoy like a floating firebomb. The master of the Royal Navy frigate *Rose* was forced to sail out into the ocean to escape her, followed by his fellow frigate, *Shark*.

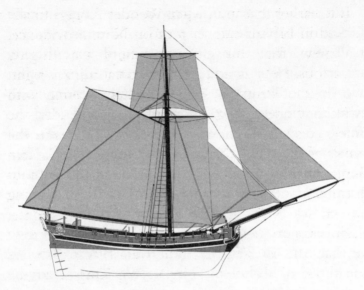

An 18th century naval sloop

Vane then fired a gun, hauled his black pirate flag up the mast and defiantly sailed out to sea under the very noses of Rogers's fleet. Then he joined Blackbeard in Oracoke Inlet, where they celebrated with a bacchanalia, an orgy of drinking, dancing and feasting. It was one of the largest gatherings of pirates ever held – but it also signalled the beginning of the end for the pirate life. For two years Charles Vane boasted that he would repay Governor Rogers for invading the pirates' haven at New Providence. But in November 1718 Blackbeard was dead, killed in a gory battle with Lieutenant Maynard of the Royal Navy, who triumphantly hung the pirate's severed head from his bowsprit.

But, earlier that year, when Woodes Rogers finally docked in Nassau and set foot on New Providence, he knew that his position there was highly precarious. He was met with an extraordinary sight: two lines of drunken, ragged pirates, swaying with drink but attempting to stand straight under the orders of some of the most notorious pirates in the annals of the Royal Navy. One of them was Captain Benjamin Hornigold, who could claim the dubious distinction of having taught Blackbeard everything he knew. Now they were a pathetic gaggle, attempting to ingratiate themselves with the new forces of the law. They fired their muskets into the air and shouted, "Hip Hip Hurrah," for King George.

At first Rogers found the island had little to offer. It appeared to be just a collection of huts, of old, leaking barrels and the squalid debris left behind by the pirates. Outside Nassau itself, the island consisted of dry and tufty scrub, low bushes flattened by the sea winds, and there were no trees. The underlying soil was an unpromising mixture of sand and dry coral. But, most importantly, there was a source of fresh water, and it soon became clear that there were enough plants to suggest that it could be made fertile for agriculture.

The fort at Nassau had nothing that would be suitable for anyone to live in, except for a few simple wooden huts. These Rogers used to house the new garrison of soldiers stationed there, to protect the island from marauding pirates who might try to take it back. To discourage the newly reformed pirates from returning to their old ways, he offered them all a small piece of land. The only condition that he made was that they must build a house on it within the year.

That summer of 1718 was a hot and stiflingly humid one. The smells of human and animal habitation hung in the air and sat heavily over the land like a tarpaulin. Most of all, the rotting hides of the cattle that the settlers had brought with them stunk horribly. They had been slaughtered in the heat, producing germs and flies, which in turn spread an epidemic of fever. It threatened to wipe out all the newcomers unused to the weather and the poor provisions. They died in their hundreds. The frigates which had escorted Rogers were called away to duties elsewhere. Only the *Rose* remained.

The ex-pirates began to grow restless. Rogers sensed that he was beginning to lose control. Pirates rarely genuinely repented. They may have claimed that they wanted to go straight, but the life of a pirate was still alluring. Though an uneasy peace reigned on New Providence, slowly but surely, one by one, the pirates left the island to return to the more lucrative business of attacking ships on the high seas.

Rogers sent three ships off to Hispaniola for provisions. But, once they were out in the open ocean, the desire for adventure overtook the crew and they reverted to their old ways. When Rogers heard that his ships were now being used for piracy, he sent Benjamin Hornigold, once a feared pirate himself but now the Governor's trusted second-in-command, to capture them and bring them back. Thirteen of the men were returned to Nassau, where a court of eight judges was established to try them.

The Governor needed to show his strength if he was to regain control of New Providence, and he was ruthless. Nine of the men were condemned to hang. Two days later, they went to the gallows at the foot of the fortress, a sign of the Governor's new determination to root out cheating pirates. He had offered them a pardon and he would make them stick to their side of the bargain. Drunk but still rebellious, some of the pirates tried for a last minute reprieve, but Rogers was firm in his resolve. They hung there for several days on the gibbet in the open, under the hot sun, as a warning to anyone else who might be tempted to follow their example.

But Rogers also realized that the old pirate order was slowly breaking down. Later that summer, Charles Vane was discovered starving with his men on an uninhabited island near Honduras in Central America. They had been shipwrecked following Vane's conviction by his own crew for cowardice, after he ordered his men to back down before a well-armed French ship. He reportedly died in "agonies" when he was caught and hung. Shortly after that came the news of the death of the infamous and apparently indestructible Blackbeard.

Blackbeard's death – more than anything else – marked the end of piracy in the Caribbean. There were a few small skirmishes, but the Golden Age, when Blackbeard and his like had ruled the seas, was gone now. In the end, Rogers even managed to make a patriotic army out of the New Providence pirates – against a common enemy, the Spanish. In January 1720, fearing an attack, he persuaded the former pirates to work like dogs, building a fort of 50 guns.

They waited for a month and then the Spanish came: 1300 Spanish troops in ships anchored in the open sea just outside Nassau. On the island, Rogers had only a motley band of a few soldiers, several ex-pirates and many drunks. There were 500 men in all.

But it turned out to be a victory for Rogers and his oddball army. The Spanish sent a small squadron of ships to block the entrance to the port. Amazingly, two sentries firing muskets from the walls of the garrison were enough to repel them. They retreated, hastily and in shame, and never dared make an approach to New Providence again.

But although Rogers had triumphed over the British government's two greatest enemies – the pirates and the Spanish – he got little reward for his achievements. After three years stationed in Nassau, he had received no money, no support and no supplies. He had to keep his men happy by paying their food bills out of his own money – and it cost him several thousand pounds.

Rogers returned home in 1721, apparently defeated and dejected. When he landed in England, the man who had almost single-handedly cleared the

Caribbean of its infestation of pirates was thrown into prison for debt. It wasn't until 1728, an amazing seven years later, that he was finally rehabilitated, restored to his old position, and given some recognition for the great service he had done his country.

Furthermore, he was determined not to be defeated in his mission to make the Bahamas a thriving colony, with waving, fertile fields of sugar and cotton. He got himself reappointed Governor of the Bahamas and had the Rogers family painted, proudly, by the famous London artist William Hogarth. In it, Woodes Rogers, wearing a long curling, fashionable wig, is seated on a fine throne-like chair on a promontary of New Providence; behind him a fine merchantman is anchored in the calm Nassau waters. His son William unrolls a map before his father, which illustrates the growing colony of New Providence. Mrs. Rogers, in her silk finery, is served a plate of delicious fresh Bahamian fruit for tea. But Rogers was not to see his utopian dream come true. He died after only four years back in the Bahamas, worn out by keeping peace among the unruly mob on the island and by the terrible heat scorching the barren soil.

But it was largely due to his efforts that the seas of the Caribbean were almost entirely free from the threat of pirates in the years to come.

The Pirate who Drank Tea

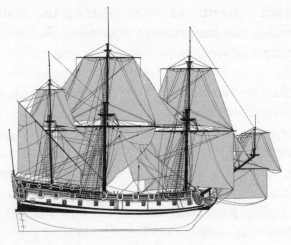

An 18th century British battleship

In 1719, a Welshman named Bartholomew Roberts was the third mate on a slaving galley named the *Princess*. He was thirty-seven years old – at that time considered well into middle age. Roberts had been at sea for over thirty years. He was a dark-haired man, unusually quiet among the noisy rabble of sailors. Still more unusually, he rarely drank alcohol, preferring to down large tankards of strong tea. But he was trusted and respected by every man who ever worked with him: he could read and write and he was renowned for making intelligent conversation.

He was musical too and, if he was in the right mood, he would sing a fine Welsh ballad. Above all, after so many years at sea, he was a master of all the skills that a sailor needed on board ship. He could navigate, he knew how to manage a crew, and he had become an expert in the tactics of naval warfare from his time aboard a Royal Navy ship during the Wars of the Spanish Succession. Bartholomew Roberts was a master mariner.

As the *Princess* slowly made her way around the shores of the Gold Coast, on the West coast of Africa, a night mist obscured the sea. The watch could see only the light on the black waters immediately below. Then, out of the gloom, he could just make out a large shape approaching at speed. It was a ship, lit up. As she drew nearer he saw, with a sickening heart, that it was bearing the *Jolly Roger*, the flag with the skull and crossbones.

There was nothing the captain of the *Princess* could do. It seemed safer to make no resistance but to hope only that the pirates would take what they wanted and leave again quickly. The pirates clambered aboard, and herded the crew together in a corner of the deck. There they watched the two pirate mother ships approach to get a better view of their prey.

"It's the *Royal Rover*," said one sailor.

"That's the ship that belongs to Howell Davies" said another. "He's a Welshman, like you, Bartholomew. You'll be getting special treatment."

"I'll be going with Davies," said the first mate. "I'm turning pirate if I have the chance. If I can take home to England a fraction of what a pirate can earn in a year, I'll be a happy man."

Roberts was silent. He watched the pirate captain climb on board to inspect his prize. There was not much in the hold for him to take, but the ship itself would be useful. And he always needed more men, so he was all too pleased to take the crew members too. Some of them wanted to try their luck at piracy – the others he would drop off at the nearest port.

The pirates didn't weigh anchor for several weeks. And, during that time, Howell Davies took a particular interest in the quiet, intelligent third mate, his fellow countryman. Davies admired his skill, the way he knew the workings of a sailing ship like the back of his own hand.

One day, Roberts was drinking a jar of tea on deck when the pirate captain approached. He sat down.

"Why don't you sail with us, Roberts?" he said.

"I haven't made my mind up," the third mate replied.

"Come on man," said Davies quietly. "You really want to go on here as third mate? It's only men with better connections than you who get to be second or first mates – let alone captain. And yet you have more skill in one little finger than they have all together."

Roberts remained silent.

"Think about it carefully, Bartholomew," said Davies, "you could be a pirate captain when you can never be more than a 'legitimate' third mate."

Soon afterwards, when the ships docked at Princes' Island, they were ambushed by the Portuguese authorities and Howell Davis was killed in the fray. The pirate ships immediately retreated into the open ocean. There, as was the custom with pirates, they held an open election for a new captain - with everyone entitled to a vote. It was Bartholomew Roberts they elected. This time, Roberts did not have to think for long.

Accepting the job, his only comment was that it would be a merry life and a short one. It seemed that it was the thought of commanding a ship, rather than a life of piracy, that initially appealed to him. But Roberts nonetheless took to the pirates' desperate and dangerous life as if he were born to it. With his leadership skills and his seamanship, he became not only a captain, but the greatest and most successful pirate captain that ever lived.

Bartholomew Roberts liked the style of captain and it suited him. The members of the pirate crew, who were used to being able to vote their captains out of a job if it suited them, respected him. He had style too. He liked to distinguish himself from the rank and file by wearing damask waistcoats in crimson (stolen, of course), a flamboyant red feather in his hat and a diamond cross on a gold chain around his neck. He kept his pair of pistols in a blue silk sling over his shoulders. Even his terrified victims conceded he had the manners of a gentleman.

Roberts's first act showed his mettle as a real

pirate. He returned to Princes' Island, where Howell Davies had been killed, and ordered his men to attack and destroy the Portuguese settlement there, in an act of revenge. He understood right from the beginning the importance of striking fear into his victims, as well as respect in the hard-grained pirates who were now under his command.

Roberts was a pirate for a scant four years, but in that short time he captured an astonishing 400 ships in a career that covered the whole of the Atlantic Ocean – from the African coast to the Caribbean. He was regarded as the emperor of the seas and soon acquired the pirate nickname "Black Bart" – referring to his swarthy features and his ruthless ambition.

When Roberts took over the *Royal Rover*, the sailors were a violent, brawling, drunken lot. Blackstrap was the name of the drink the pirates liked best – a vile but potent brew consisting of rum, molasses and beer. Roberts couldn't prevent them from drinking – it was one of the only consolations of long weeks at sea eating nothing but biscuits. But Black Bart was a man of discipline – a quarter of a century in the Royal Navy had taught him that you couldn't successfully govern a group of men working on a ship without firm rules. So he drew up some regulations of his own, which he called his "Articles".

All pirate ships had regulations. Contrary to what many people imagine, life on a pirate ship was not free and easy; like the regular Navy, pirates recognized the need for rules to keep order on board.

Roberts's articles were not dramatically different, but he knew the value of a rule of law and he intended to make these rules particularly his own. There would be absolutely no brawling – on pain of the harshest punishments that a pirate ship could adminster. There would be no women on the ships (a basic rule on almost all pirate vessels) and no candles below decks after eight o'clock at night. This was because drinking by night with candles created the biggest risk of fire; and all mariners feared fire at sea more than any other danger. Morality and strict discipline would make the *Royal Rover* and her fleet the most feared pirate fleet in the known world.

For Roberts's first real prize, the crew decided to try their luck off the coast of Brazil. There, after loitering out at sea for some time, they came across a fleet of 42 ships sailing from Brazil to Lisbon. The largest, a ship named the *Sagrada Familia*, had 40 guns and 150 men. It was considerably larger and better armed than the *Royal Rover* and was surrounded and protected by the other ships of the fleet. But this did not deter Roberts. Outgunned and outnumbered, he daringly ordered his men to fire broadsides into the flanks of the *Sagrada*. She buckled and was captured. As the pirates piled on board, they discovered the ship was laden with sugar, animal skins and tobacco – as well as thousands of pounds worth of solid gold pieces.

Roberts and his pirates withdrew with their booty to Devil's Island, a sleazy pirate hangout hundreds of miles from any other land. There they drank and gambled away their winnings – until, that is, they saw the ships of the Royal Navy approaching the island and made a swift getaway. Then they pointed their fleet north, in the direction of the American Atlantic seaboard.

Roberts carried off several other successful attacks and, in June 1720, with no more than 60 men accompanying him in a sloop of only 10 guns, Black Bart attacked the port of Trepanny in Newfoundland in North America. This was the attack that made Roberts famous.

There were 22 ships anchored in Trepanny – most of them merchantmen – and 1200 men, as well as 40 cannons and 150 fishing vessels. By sheer defiant bravado, Roberts took them all, every single one. Then he went on to plunder the port and sink several of the ships just for fun. The people of Trepanny didn't fire a single shot to defend themselves. Even the Governor of New England, when he heard of the attack, had to admit that Bartholomew Roberts was a pirate of rare skill and bravery.

"One cannot withold admiration for his courage and daring," he wrote. But there were also reports that Roberts's crew had brutally tortured the men they found in their way, slitting off their ears. There were others that they had tied to the yardarm and fired at. "Black Bart" had earned his nickname.

It was on this occasion that Roberts used music to strike fear and confusion in his victims. He was to become well known for this tactic, often forcing professional musicians, to join his company and take part in the raids. The attack on Trepanny was accompanied by "drums beating, trumpets sounding, and other instruments of music, the English flag flying, the pirate flag at the topmast head with death's head and cutlass" - so said a report in the *Boston News Letter.*

Bartholomew Roberts loved music. When he captured musicians, he would insist (and he even made it a rule in one of his Articles) that they play every day except Sundays - and for as long, and whenever, he commanded. It was the tea-drinking pirate's only indulgence.

Roberts took on more hands in Trepanny. Newoundland was a famous recruiting ground for pirates. The grinding misery of the cod-fishing industry in that wet, cloudy patch of North America meant there were a lot of willing recruits to the pirate's life. He also took possession of a Bristol galley that was moored there to be his flagship, renaming it the *Royal Fortune.* No ship's name could have been more appropriate than the *Royal Fortune's.* For Bartholomew Roberts was about to embark on four years of almost unbroken success and riches.

After leaving Trepanny, Roberts scooped up every ship that lay in his path. From one, a sloop named the *Samuel,* his men stole sails, guns, powder, rigging and over £10,000 worth of goods. His men had already made an average of £700 each - which would be worth over £100,000 (nearly $200,000) today.

By September 1720, Roberts had returned to the Caribbean, where he intended to pick up fresh water and provisions before heading back across the Atlantic to Africa. About halfway there, he found the wind pushing him back north and he was forced to return to the Caribbean. Then he had to return across the Atlantic Ocean without stopping. His ships only had 63 gallons (known as a hogshead) of water to last 124 men. The days became weeks, waiting for the weather to turn and sweep them back to land. The pirates were only permitted one small mouthful of water every 24 hours and some were driven to drinking their own urine. A few even drank sea water – which, as all sailors know, is the surest way to madness, because salt water only gives you an insatiable thirst which kills you in the end. But at last they saw land – it was Surinam in South America. A boat was launched and returned with brackish river water. But it was just in time. Altogether it had been a terrifying trip of 2,000 miles.

Once fortified and strengthened, the *Royal Fortune* and her fleet launched a furious raiding campaign in the Caribbean. The speed and efficiency of the pirates' attacks surpassed anything that had been seen before. The trading vessels were powerless before Black Bart and his men. Roberts sailed boldly into all the major ports and picked off hundreds of ships at a time. The Governor of the Leeward Islands reported to his government that in three days (between October 28-31, 1720) the pirates seized, burned or sank 15 French and English vessels and one Dutch.

Map of South America, showing Surinam,
where Black Bart launched his attack on the Caribbean

Roberts prowled the waters of the island of St. Lucia like a shark, picking off ships coming in from Martinique and Barbados. By the end of 1721, there was virtually no shipping moving in the Caribbean at all. Roberts had brought trading to a standstill.

He had the ruling colonial governments of the Caribbean by the nose - and he knew it. After 25 years as a junior seaman, answering to men who were less skilled and knowledgeable than himself, now

Bartholomew Roberts could call the shots.

He wrote the Governor of the Leeward Islands this mocking letter:

Gentlemen,
This comes expressly from me to lett you know that had you come off as you ought to a done and drank a Glass of wine with me and my company I sould not harmed the least vessell in your harbour. Further it is not your guns you fired that affrighted me or hindered our coming ashore, but the wind not proving to our expectation.

Roberts himself, ever the dandy, enjoyed watching the feeble efforts of the authorities to chase and capture him. Apart from his well-known pennant, which showed a captain and a skeleton drinking a toast to death, Roberts was soon flying a flag of his own design. It bore a picture of Black Bart himself wielding a sword, with his feet on two skulls. Underneath were inscribed letters that would strike a chill into the hearts of any Caribbean sailor: ABH (A Barbadian's Head) and AMH (A Martinician's Head). On his cabin door he stuck a plate with the same design. In four years, the quiet, thoughtful sailor had become a violent, vain, bloodthirsty pirate king, with a taste for flamboyant mockery.

The *Royal Fortune* set back out again for Africa and landed at Senegal on the west coast. From there, they careened and refitted their ships in Sierra Leone, where they were welcomed by the English traders who were based there. There was nothing like the sight of a pirate ship on the horizon to get the taverns open and everyone carousing happily. Everybody knew that there was no bigger spender of money than a pirate. Many of the traders had seen the Royal Navy men-of-war patrolling the coast, armed with 60 guns each, on the lookout for Black Bart and the *Royal Fortune*. But Roberts, drinking tea that night on the *Royal Fortune* while intently studying his charts, thought he could afford to overlook the presence of a couple of men-of-war. It was his first major mistake. But it was a fatal one.

In August 1721, Bartholomew Roberts set sail towards the African country which is now named Liberia. He captured a frigate, the *Onslow*, and changed her name to the one that had brought him such spectacular good luck before - another *Royal Fortune*. On they sailed, plundering everything that came across their path, until they reached the mouth of the Calabar River. Filthy, insect-infested, disease-ridden and humid, the river was full of tiny creeks: the perfect pirate hiding place. But their fights with local tribes were so vicious that the name of Bartholomew Roberts is still remembered in the histories of the local people of Old Calabar.

By mid-December, Black Bart had worked his way up the West African coast and by January 11 the following year, he sailed into Ouidah, the most powerful slaving port on the entire coast. He went right past Cape Castle, where the Navy's men-of-war were stationed. Roberts, who had wrongly calculated that they had already sailed on to Sierra Leone, was unaware that they were there. But they saw the *Royal Fortune* only too well – and set after her.

The pirates then received a message from an ally on the mainland saying that Captain Chaloner Ogle was pursuing them in the *Swallow*. Roberts put to sea and headed for the tiny island of Annobon, a speck miles away in the middle of the Indian Ocean. But the winds were against him. The pirate fleet arrived at Cape Lopez instead and went into hiding in the myriad inlets around the Cape. Secretly, Captain Ogle and the *Swallow* crept in behind them. Luckily for them, they heard a shot which alerted them to the presence of *Royal Fortune*.

Then Roberts made his second mistake. From the distance, he thought the *Swallow* was a merchant ship, a potentially juicy prize. So he ordered the *Great Ranger*, one of the smaller ships in his fleet, to set off in pursuit of her. Captain Ogle, thinking quickly, decided to dupe him. He headed back towards the open sea as if he was fleeing the pirates. The *Great Ranger* followed him and, when they were out of earshot of the rest of the fleet, Ogle allowed the ship to gain on him slowly As the pirates approached, ready with muskets and cutlasses to swing themselves into the *Swallow*, Ogle turned his ship around and surprised them with a broadside, a heavy blast of fire from all the cannons on one side of his ship, that tore into the side of the *Great Ranger*.

By the time the Navy officers came aboard, the *Great Ranger* was blackened, charred and peppered with holes. On the deck, dozens of pirates lay wounded and crying out; about ten of them were dead. The *Swallow* suffered not a single casualty. Ogle then took his ship into Cape Lopez, to force an encounter with Roberts and his two remaining ships.

It was February 10, early in the morning, and Roberts was breakfasting on salmagundi, that toxic pirate dish which consists of nothing but meat and strong spices boiled for many hours into an oily, fiery porridge. He was already on his second pint of tea. His men were bleary and hung over after a night's boozing and they were hardly fit to stand, let alone to fight. When word came to Roberts that the *Swallow* had destroyed the *Great Ranger* and was now heading their way, he must have known that his career as a pirate was about to end.

Looking around at his men, he realized at a glance that they weren't up to a battle and decided that the *Royal Fortune* should make a run for it. He ordered the crew to go full sail. Then he put on his feathered hat, slung his silken rope of pistols around his shoulders and his diamond cross around his neck. The *Royal Fortune* was heading at full speed away from the *Swallow* when Roberts, in a final act of bravado, ordered his men to turn the ship around and face down the enemy.

As the two ships opened fire on each other, Roberts was seen slumped on a gun carriage, his neck later found to be gaping like a sieve with dozens of grapeshot holes. After four triumphant years of piracy, Black Bart was dead. His men, many of them weeping, threw him overboard in his fine coat and hat. It was how he wanted it to be: a sailor's burial.

Roberts's men lost heart when they lost his leadership. On board the *Royal Fortune* everything descended into chaos. By 7 o' clock that evening, the fighting was over. Roberts's three ships, the *Royal Fortune*, the *Great Ranger* and the *Little Ranger*, had been completely overcome and were blasted with holes.

More than 200 pirate prisoners were taken to Cape Coast Castle in irons and clapped together in an underground dungeon cut into the rocks below the fortress. Bartholomew Roberts's original crew, proud of having served under such a famous villain, considered themselves a cut above the rest of the prisoners. They referred to themselves as the House of Lords.

When the trial finally came, it was the biggest of its kind that had ever been seen. Of the English pirates, 20 died before the trial began, and 18 Frenchmen were acquitted because they could not answer charges in an English court. The remaining 169 men appeared in the dock to defend themselves against the charge of piracy on the high seas.

Of all those who were tried, 52 were executed. They hanged them in batches – and it took two weeks to complete the work. A quarter of the bodies were dipped in tar and hung on gibbets overlooking the coast, where they dried quickly in the sun: a warning to anyone contemplating a pirate's life.

The death of Black Bart brought to an end the great days of piracy. He was the last and the greatest pirate captain. The news of his death was greeted with relief by governments all over the world – from the Americas to India and Africa. Wherever nations traded by sea, there was celebration at the news of the death of Bartholomew Roberts.

As for Captain Chaloner Ogle, he was knighted. He was the only naval officer ever to receive this distinction for bringing a pirate to justice. He had taken on Black Bart and he had won.

Captain Kidd: the Reluctant Pirate

Captain Kidd's ship, the Adventure Galley

In the countryside around New York, it is said that the ghost of Captain Kidd sometimes visits remote farmhouses. The weary sailor, his clothes wet with salt water, knocks on doors to ask the way to Wall Street. He always offers to pay for a night's lodging with a strange gold coin which appears to have come from the region around the Red Sea.

Poor Captain Kidd - not even at peace when he is dead. In life, he became the most famous of all pirates, synonymous with legends of buried treasure.

In England, in the 18th century, people sang songs to frighten children about wicked Captain William Kidd, the once law-abiding clergyman's son who had buried the family Bible before he embarked on a murderous career as a pirate. For years, Captain Kidd's hanged body, left to dangle in its rusting metal cage above the docks at Tilbury, served as the deadliest warning to any sailor contemplating life as a pirate.

But Captain Kidd was probably the most misunderstood man in the history of piracy. He was one of the most reluctant and unsuccessful of pirates, and certainly not the most evil. Of all the pirates in the Golden Age, he probably spilled the least blood. Kidd, who was a middle-aged man with a prosperous career behind him, did not mean to become a pirate at all. In fact, he set out to be a pirate-catcher.

At the age of nearly fifty, William Kidd was a respected merchant, a wealthy citizen of the new city of New York and a friend of the Governor. He had married a rich woman and had two daughters. Once or twice a year, he made trading runs between London and New York in his sloop, *Antegoa*. It was on one of these runs, in 1694, that he met a New Yorker named Robert Livingston who had a money-making scheme that he thought would interest Kidd.

Livingston suggested that Kidd might like to join with him in a project that might help deter pirates in the Red Sea, while also ensuring a tidy profit for himself. The idea was to fit up a ship that would capture pirate vessels. It would be backed by prominent and wealthy men who would be promised a huge return on their investment – from the plundered treasure that would be recovered on the pirates' ships. After all, there would be nothing illegal in taking loot that had already been stolen from other ships, would there?

During the 1690s, the Eastern Seas – the Indian Ocean, the Red Sea and the Arabian Sea – were swarming with fleets of pirate ships. They had their pick of the choicest of the East India Company's wealthy trading ships that were busy transporting goods to England from India. But the rulers of India threatened to cut off trading links, unless the British government could do something about the pirate threat. The government was at its wits' end.

Livingston managed to arrange a meeting with Lord Bellomont at the peer's London home. Lord Bellomont had just been appointed Governor of New York and he listened to their plan with interest. Then he sent two agents to see four of England's most powerful men, friends of King William III and themselves influential politicians: the Earl of Romney, the Earl of Orford, the Duke of Shrewsbury and Sir John Somers. They asked that their names be kept out of the public eye, of course. But when they heard of the potential rewards that might be theirs from captured pirate vessels, they were more than happy to put large sums into the project.

Between them, the four men put up £6,000, four-fifths of the amount needed for the venture, and Livingston and Kidd together put up the final fifth.

Kidd was commissioned to hunt down pirate ships and bring home their stolen cargoes. But he also received two official letters giving him permission to attack any ship belonging to France – as France was England's enemy at the time. The King himself wrote a special royal letter of commission, in exchange for one tenth of the plunder – though, of course, he insisted that this never be made public. It gave Kidd the authority to seize pirate ships – and to confiscate their merchandizes and their money.

Bellomont and his friends were determined to extract a profit from the enterprise and so they reassured Captain Kidd that they would stand by him, no matter what happened. Kidd had always been easily impressed by people in positions of influence and he was completely confident that these official letters gave him personal, royal protection. He proudly considered himself on the King's business. But Kidd's confidence was seriously misplaced.

Livingston and the English noblemen were delighted with the prospect of their future riches. It was surely a watertight plan – not only would it net them a great deal of money, but it would be seen as a fine public service. And William Kidd, that honest, reliable, sea captain, with his long experience of pirates from his days serving his country in the Navy, seemed just the man for the job.

But, while they were fitting out the ship for its voyage to the Eastern Seas, Captain Kidd began to get cold feet. He would have to sell his own ship in order to raise the money he needed, and he began to wonder if the chances of catching a French ship in the Indian Ocean, let alone a pirate ship carrying sufficient treasure, were too small to repay his investment. He also had nagging doubts about his own position. Ships didn't always fly their country's flags, so what would happen if he attacked a ship that was flying a French flag but turned out not to be French? What if he didn't manage to catch a pirate ship? And if he did capture a ship – didn't that make Kidd a pirate too?

Captain Kidd's ship, the *Adventure Galley*, was launched at Deptford in 1695, about a year later. It was a formidable vessel of 287 tons with 34 guns. Kidd chose his crew carefully. His first consideration was that they shouldn't be likely to run off and join the pirates themselves. This was a serious risk – as the rewards of a life of piracy, however brief, far outweighed the paltry wages of a regular sailor. So Kidd deliberately chose men who were married and settled and had good reason to want to come home again. The men were also promised 25% between them of any booty that was taken. Livingston and Kidd were to take 15% and their wealthy backers were to clean up the remaining 60%.

The first calamity occurred on the first day of sailing. For reasons that he never made clear, Kidd refused to salute a Royal Navy yacht at Greenwich, just outside London. The yacht responded by firing into the air to remind him to show due respect, whereupon Kidd's crew all turned and slapped their backsides in an insolent manner. Kidd had made an enemy of the Navy before he had even reached the open sea. Shortly after that unfortunate episode, a Royal Navy press gang boarded the ship and pressed nearly all Kidd's crew off the ship and forced them to work in the King's fleet. They were replaced by a band of hopeless misfits rejected even by the Navy.

Bad luck or bad judgement? Captain Kidd certainly had plenty of both. But his character almost guaranteed his unpopularity with his men. For Kidd was difficult to like: though he was a competent and respected seaman, he was pompous and could be a bully. He liked to show off about his grand connections and affected a self-important swagger. For the next six years, Kidd would struggle to keep in control of the motley collection of desperadoes under his command – and eventually it would bring about his ruin.

Seven months after the incident in the Thames, *Adventure Galley* reached New York, where Kidd immediately set about looking for new crew members. As most of the sailors loitering around the city docks had at one time been pirates, they were not enthusiastic about signing up for a voyage with a mission to catch pirates. In desperation, Kidd was forced to raise the stakes. He offered potential crewmen an amazing 60% of any booty captured. But he omitted to inform his wealthy partners back in England of his decision – and this would come back to haunt him later.

Captain Kidd eventually assembled 150 unruly criminals and prepared to set sail on *Adventure Galley*. He was all too aware that if he didn't come up with the promised spoils they were likely to turn on him. Colonel Fletcher, the Governor of New York who was about to be replaced by Lord Bellomont, wrote of Kidd's expedition: *"Many flocked to him from all parts, men of desperate fortunes and necessities, in expectaton of getting vast treasure. It is generally believed here that if he misses the design named in his commission, he will not be able to govern such a villainous herd."*

From New York, the *Adventure Galley* sailed to Madagascar – a voyage of five months. Kidd, proudly waving his royal commission, arrogantly demanded some new sails from a Royal Navy squadron stationed there. He said that if they didn't hand them over he would send some of his crew to seize them. At Johanna Island in the Indian Ocean, where he stopped to make some repairs to the ship, he met an East Indiaman flying the Royal Navy flag. Captain Kidd officiously ordered him to take it down, on the grounds that he alone, with his royal commission, was entitled to fly the royal flag. In the world of sailors and seaports, where news travels quickly, Captain Kidd had made himself a reputation as an annoying, puffed-up and altogether slightly ridiculous figure.

Kidd's bad luck did not run out. After Johanna, he went to the island of Mehila in the Comoros, off the east coast of Africa. There, in one single week, 50 of his men died of dysentry and disease. The remaining crew began to mutter discontentedly; many of them threatened to join the pirates unless some of the money they'd been promised materialized quickly. The atmosphere was stinking hot and humid, there was very little food to go around, and tempers were dangerously frayed.

In July 1697, Captain Kidd dropped anchor at the small island of Perim at the mouth of the Red Sea. With its traffic of Arab dhows and Indian merchant ships, this was a popular pirates' ambush spot: surely he would find a ship to capture here? Kidd sent a boat across the straits to the port of Mocha to gather information on ships passing through. They reported back that a fleet of 15 Moorish ships, from Morocco and North Africa, were about to sail right past Perim. But there was no sign of any pirate ships.

The *Adventure Galley* lurked there for three weeks, waiting. The weather was burning hot and wet, and the humidity made movement almost impossible. Kidd must by now have deeply regretted the whole expedition into which he had sunk his reputation and his life's savings. His royal commission seemed now to be worth very little - and certainly not to a crew maddened to the point of violence through hunger and frustration. Kidd dared not go home empty-handed, he was so deeply in debt with his investment in the *Adventure Galley*. He knew that he had to capture a prize, but there were no French or pirate ships available to him. If he didn't come back with something, his crew would mutiny and he and his family would die in poverty.

Kidd then made a decision that was to prove fatal to him. He decided to attack the Moorish fleet. It was true that many Christian governments turned a blind-eye to the looting of Arab ships – although of course it was still piracy – and Kidd must have been hoping that the wealthy lords back home would do the same.

Captain Kidd had never wanted to be a pirate. Far from it. He was an upstanding citizen, not an anarchic criminal. But his men were baying for blood and money. And – after all – these ships did not belong to England's allies (though many of them were flying Dutch or English flags). But they were escorted by several well-armed British East Indiamen.

On August 14, the Moorish fleet finally sailed out of Mocha and the *Adventure Galley* went after it. There are conflicting stories about what really happened next – but it seems the ships opened fire on Kidd and he replied by firing back. He had no wish to identify himself and flew no country's flag – only a plain red pennant.

The master of *Sceptre*, one of the convoy of British East Indiamen, waited until the *Adventure Galley* drew alongside the largest of the merchant ships, then opened all *Sceptre*'s guns into her. Kidd's vessel took a hit in the hull and was forced to retreat, with the *Sceptre* giving chase.

Captain Kidd's first foray into piracy had been a disaster. He'd been chased off at the first attempt.

Now his men began to treat him with open disrespect. Gradually, he gave way to their demands, allowing them to board a small Moorish barque off the coast of southern India which had an English captain. But they came away with nothing but a bale of pepper and a sack of coffee. Kidd then forced the English captain – whose name was Parker – to join him as a pilot. His expert knowledge of the local waters would aid with navigation. He also took on board the Portuguese mate to help with the language.

Ironically, by the time Captain Kidd stopped at the Indian port of Karwar, his reputation for piracy had arrived before him. Two English officers boarded the *Adventure Galley* and demanded the release of Captain Parker and his mate. Typically, instead of having the good sense to brave it out, Kidd locked the men in the hold and furiously denied their existence to the officers.

Although the word was now going around the trading stations that Kidd was a rough and brutal captain, who inspired respect among his men because of his royal commision, the truth was that Kidd's men had the upper hand. They were continually arguing among themselves and there was brooding unease and restlessness on board. To keep them from mutiny, Kidd had to resort to giving in to their demands When the ship moored in the Laccadive Islands, the crew went ashore where they beat up the villagers, chopped down the local trees for firewood and burned down a village. When the news of their misconduct spread, it was Kidd who was blamed.

But Kidd still maintained that he was a proud servant of the King, waving his now useless commission under the nose of anyone who tried to question it. Even in the face of disaster, he still blindly hoped to carry out the demands of his sponsors. Surely they would be grateful to him, he reasoned, when he returned with a hold full of treasure and his reputation as a public servant restored.

But by the time the *Adventure Galley* left Karwar, she had a acquired a reputation as a pirate ship and the local East India Company officer refused to give Kidd supplies. Captain Kidd was now completely isolated.

Two months later, after a fruitless cruise across an empty ocean, the *Adventure Galley* came in sight of a cargo ship. The crew, excited by the prospect of a fat prize, drew the ship in closer. But, as they did so, it became clear that the cargo ship, the *Loyal Captain*, was flying an English flag. Many of his men wanted to plunder the ship immediately, but Kidd was outraged. He refused even to think of it. But he knew he was already compromised. As they drew alongside the ship, the crew threatened mutiny, but Kidd managed to hold firm. In his own eyes at least, as long as he left English ships alone, he was still an upstanding patriot and not a pirate.

But the crew seethed resentfully belowdecks, led by a gunner named William Moore. Moore taunted Kidd that they could have taken the *Loyal Captain* and no one would have been any the wiser.

"You've brought us to ruin," he scoffed contemptuously.

Kidd lost his temper completely and screamed at him, "You lousy dog!"

In his rage, he brought a bucket crashing down on Moore's head. It was leather, but ringed in solid iron. The gunner fell to the ground, bleeding from a fractured skull; the next morning he was dead. The crew watched these proceedings with silent fury. After they had disposed of Moore's coffin over the side of the ship, they went about their chores sullenly. Kidd was living on borrowed time- and he knew it.

Several weeks went by before the *Adventure Galley* claimed what Kidd could call their first "legitimate" prize. The *Maiden* was skippered by a Dutchman and crewed by Moors. But, as Kidd's ship drew alongside, the captain showed Kidd a French pass. Kidd immediately took this to be a sign that they were within their rights to seize its cargo of cotton, quilts and sugar – which they did. He sold the plunder on the Indian coast for cash and gold, which he then shared out among the men to keep them quiet. This was directly disobeying the rules of his contract, but Kidd knew that to let the crew have nothing from this, their first prize, would be tempting violence. So he kept the *Maiden*, renamed her *November*, and took her along with *Adventure Galley*.

It was not always possible to identify exactly a ship's nationality, as captains often carried many different passes, each belonging to a different nation and each useful in different waters. What Kidd did not know – or could not afford to ask – was that the owner of the *Maiden* was Indian, and not French, which meant that Kidd had committed piracy. But his most pressing concern was no longer the rules of the project on which he had been employed, but the need to pacify his men with blood and gold.

This first act of piracy began Kidd's downward spiral. From then on, other ships fell prey to the *Adventure Galley*. First, it was another Moorish ship, and then, more dangerously, a Portuguese one. Often the spoils of the attack added up to little more than a few sacks of coffee and some bags of rice. But, on January 30, 1698, Kidd came across an altogether larger prize.

The *Quetta Merchant* was a 500-ton merchantman belonging to Armenians and captained by an Englishman named Wright. It was on its way from Bengal in the east of India, to Surat in the west, with a cargo of silks, muslins, sugar, iron, guns and gold. Kidd spotted her just off the South Indian coast by the port of Cochin. The *Adventure Galley* pursued her for four hours. Kidd ran up a French flag in the hope that the *Quetta Merchant* would do the same. Captain Wright, imagining that this would protect the ship, sent up an old French gunner to pose as the captain. The gunner handed Kidd a French pass and again Kidd imagined he had a legitimate prize,

He sold the cargo on the coast for and again

divided up the money between the crew. Then he sailed towards Africa and the island of Madagascar. Only five weeks into the journey, Captain Wright's true identity was revealed. When Kidd discovered, to his horror, that he had taken an English captain prisoner, he realized he had stepped so far over the rules, there was no going back. In desperation, he summoned the crew onto the deck and proposed giving back the *Quetta Merchant* to Captain Wright and letting it go free. But the crew wouldn't hear of it. So, as Kidd dared not risk offending them, the three ships sailed on towards Madagascar – an island virtually controlled by pirates.

It was, appropriately, April Fools' Day, 1698, when the three ships approached Madagascar, entering through the pirates' haven of St. Mary's Island where, for the first time, Kidd, the erstwhile pirate-catcher, encountered a real pirate ship, the *Mocha Frigate*. It had been captured by pirate captain Robert Culliford some weeks before and was now anchored in the bay.

Still keen to do his duty, Kidd urged his men to seize the ship while it was at anchor. But they simply laughed in his face. They would rather kill him, they mocked, than kill a pirate. Then all but thirteen of them promptly deserted him to join Culliford's crew. As if that wasn't enough, they set fire to the *November*, took with them anything of value in the three ships and burned Kidd's log book. He had to barricade himself in his cabin. It was his last humiliation. He would never be able to claw back his authority with his men again.

After weeks locked up in his cabin, Kidd surrendered. He swore that he would never do the pirate chief Culliford any harm. Culliford, finding the pompous captain completely in his control, magnanimously spared his life. Culliford's *Mocha* then sailed triumphantly out of St. Mary's, with three-quarters of Kidd's crew on board and a new arsenal of guns looted from Kidd's fleet.

Kidd decided to return home in the *Quetta Merchant*. The *Adventure Galley* was finished now. Wrecked and lying lopsided on a sandbank, she was past repair. Ever optimistic, he still believed he was carrying enough treasure left over from his sporadic raids to satisfy his sponsors back at home. There might even be a little left over for himself. And he had kept the two French passes in case awkward questions were asked. Even Captain Kidd could not have imagined that he had kept to the rules of his commissions to the letter – but in his own mind he had kept them well enough.

What Kidd didn't know was that the East India Company had written a letter to the Lords Justices in London, in which they made some strongly-worded charges of piracy against him. Back in England, it had become clear to Kidd's backers that the whole scheme had been a failure and – what was worse for them – an embarrassing failure. The newspapers were calling for answers from those who had sponsored this crazy expedition. The sponsors no longer wanted to be associated with Kidd's exploits – preferring to cut loose altogether. And they needed a scapegoat.

The Lords gave a naval squadron on its way to the Indian Ocean the urgent task of capturing of Captain Kidd. At the same time, they wrote to the governors of the American colonies, ordering them to apprehend Kidd so that, in the words of their letter, *"he and his associates be prosecuted with the utmost rigour of the law."*

Suddenly Kidd, the hapless fool, the self-important pirate-hunter, the friend of men in high places, was the archenemy. Without realizing it, he had become the pirate cut-throat of popular imagination. He was guilty in the eyes of the English public before he had even set foot back on his native soil.

Kidd only discovered how perilous his position was when he reached the Caribbean and sent a boat ashore to the island of Anguilla. It returned with the devastating news that, in every known port, Kidd and those men who had remained with him had been declared pirates. The orders were that they were to be arrested and put in chains on sight.

Kidd paused to consider his position. Many of the men wanted to run for it, to split up and make their own way into hiding. But Kidd longed to return home. He remembered his large and comfortable house in New York, his respectable family, his wife and two daughters. They too would suffer if he were disgraced. So he determined to brave it out and go to New York to make a deal with Lord Bellomont, who was now the city's governor.

First of all, he had to get rid of the *Quetta Merchant*, which was too large and conspicuous. He bought a smaller sloop, the *Antonio*, from its skipper just off the coast of the island of Hispaniola, and unloaded much of the *Quetta Merchant*'s treasure into the hold. Then, with a crew of only twelve men, the rest having chosen to lie low with the *Quetta Merchant*, he sailed to New York to try his luck.

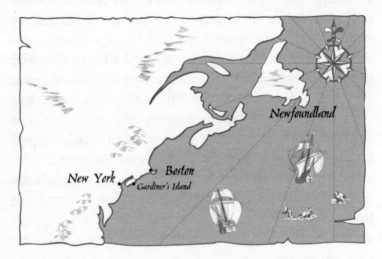

Map of the northeast coast of America, where Captain Kidd began - and ended - his expedition

Kidd anchored the *Antonio* in Oyster Bay, Long Island. Using an old lawyer friend of his, James Emmott, he sent a message to Lord Bellomont asking him to come out to the ship. He also sent him the two French passes - proof, he thought, that he had only been obeying orders when he plundered the *Quetta Merchant* and the *Maiden*.

Bellomont decided to inveigle Captain Kidd into stepping ashore. He sent him a letter suggesting that if Kidd was to come in he could be given a King's pardon. Kidd, always ready to trust the word of his aristocratic friends, was easily persuaded – though he was canny enough to shore up his bargaining tools by burying some of his valuables in the sandy soil of Gardiner's Island, in Long Island Sound. He even got a receipt from the island's owner, so that he could retrieve it when he returned – as he was confident he would.

Unwisely Kidd also tried to bribe influential people in New York by sending them gifts of gold, silk and other treasures. This only infuriated the Governor, who saw Kidd using the spoils of the expedition that he, Lord Bellomont, had helped finance, as if it were his own personal property.

For two happy weeks, Kidd's wife and daughters joined him on the *Antonio*. He had been away from home for three years. Kidd reassured them that he would be found not guilty, that it was all a mistake, that he would be protected by Lord Bellomont and King William himself. But now even Kidd was beginning to realize that his position was precarious. He decided to sail to Boston and demand a meeting with Lord Bellomont, who was now based there. Foolishly, to sweeten his request, he sent a green silk bag of gold bars to Lady Bellomont – who immediately sent them back.

The authorities were now weary of the chase and issued an order for his arrest. Captain Kidd was finally captured standing before Lord Bellomont's front door, hammering desperately to be let in. In front of the very man who had ordered him to sea, he drew his sword in desperation before he was overcome. Lord Bellomont watched impassively as Kidd was dragged off, shouting his innocence.

They threw him into a stinking cell, in solitary confinement, locked in irons that weighed sixteen pounds. The officials searched desperately for Kidd's reputedly fabulous treasure, rounding up all the gifts and bribes and ordering John Gardiner to hand over the hoard that was buried on his island. Everything they found was shipped under close guard to London and the Treasury coffers.

Kidd was despatched to London, along with six members of his crew who were arrested later. He began to lose his mind in the stench and the freezing hold, and he begged for a knife to kill himself. When they docked on the Thames, Kidd was taken, sick and trembling, to Newgate Prison, the biggest jail in London. It was a filthy, clamorous place and he was locked up there among the villainous inmates for over a year, not even allowed to write letters to defend himself. The Admiralty had put aside a small sum to pay for his lawyers, but the lawyers never received the money and couldn't start work on his case until two hours before the trial began.

Kidd was taken from Newgate to Westminster. Members of Parliament wanted to hear about the role that Bellomont and his friends had played in his escapades – but Kidd, woozy from his ill treatment, did not perhaps understand. Perhaps (and this would have been typical of him) he thought he knew better? Instead of indicting his patrons, of explaining clearly their part in his piracy, he remained on the defensive, protesting his innocence to a group of politicians who were markedly unsympathetic. Most of them thought he was truculent; many of them just thought he was drunk.

Kidd was eventually permitted to present his case. The two vital pieces of evidence – the French passes he'd been given – had mysteriously disappeared. Kidd himself was not allowed to testify in the witness box and his lawyer was not permitted to call any of the former members of his crew to witness to his good character. Moreover, the prosecution had two star witnesses – pirates named Palmer and Bradenham, who had been among those who had deserted Kidd for Culliford in Madagascar. They testified that they had seen Kidd murder the gunner William Moore. In vain, Kidd protested that it had been an accident, but he was still found guilty. The jury also found him guilty of acts of piracy on the *Quetta* and the *Maiden* – as well as on Moorish and Portuguese ships. In their final statement, the prosecution called him, "an arch-pirate, equally cruel, dreaded and hated both on land and on sea."

All poor Kidd could do was protest his innocence and cry that he had been the victim of "perjured and wicked" people. We do not know whether any of them, Lords Orford and Romney or Sir John Summers and the Duke of Shrewsbury, were watching him in court. But they might have felt a twinge of shame as their scapegoat was sentenced to hang by the neck until dead. The log book which, Kidd pleaded, would have proved his innocence had been burned by the pirate crew when he was locked in his cabin in Madagascar.

Captain Kidd had to be drunk when they hanged him, at Execution Dock near Tilbury, on the edge of the Thames. He thanked God that some kind soul had taken pity on him and slipped him a flask of rum on the morning of his execution. He was visited by the prison chaplain who tried to press a confession out of him, but Kidd refused. His tumbril, draped in black, moved slowly through London to Hangman's Fair, where pirates were executed. All the way it was followed by crowds who screamed in delight as it passed. A hanging was always a cause for celebration, especially when it was a pirate – as condemned pirates often tossed their last remaining pieces–of–eight into the crowd. The chaplain later noted that Kidd expressed grief at leaving his wife and children, but refused to ask forgiveness or to show regret. He protested his innocence until the very end.

They had to hang him twice. On the first attempt, the rope snapped and he was flung into the mud. Dazed, the old sea captain, weak through ill-treatment and treachery, was led up the steps again. The chaplain finally exhorted from him a plea for forgiveness – though he still would not say it was for acts of piracy.

The body of Captain Kidd was left by the Thames

until the water had ebbed and flowed over it three times – as the law dictated for pirates. Then it was coated in tar, bound with chains and set in a tight metal harness. This meant that, as the flesh decayed, the bones would remain upright in their swinging cage – a fearful sight for mariners entering the docks.

Of the nine men tried with Kidd, only six were convicted of piracy and only one of those was hanged. Palmer and Bradenham received a full pardon in exchange for their evidence. The others bribed their way out of Newgate and later collected the stores of stolen gold they had buried. History does not relate whether they ever expressed remorse for their part in the terrible fate of Captain Kidd. But perhaps his seawater-sodden ghost occasionally came knocking at their doors?

Two Hell-Cats

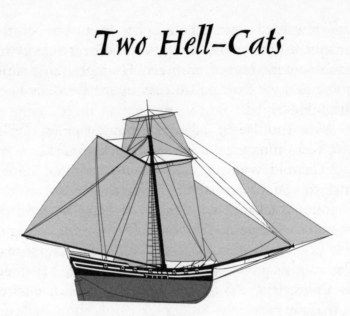

A pirate sloop

It was mid-morning and there was a buzz of expectation among the crowds who had clustered around the prison in Spanish Town, Jamaica. Most of the people there been waiting for several hours, swatting the flies which were gathering, maddeningly, under a blustery sky.

A cheer went up as the prisoners appeared. They were a raggedy collection, shuffling in their leg-irons – thin and hollow-cheeked after months of eating nothing but cold mashed beans and greasy pork fat in their dirty cells.

"It's Calico Jack," said one of the crowd.

"Hey, Jack," cried a toothless old woman among the spectators. "Hey Jack, gissa kiss Calico Jack." She was rewarded with a wan grin from one of the prisoners, distinguishable from the others only by his grubby, wide-legged trousers. Through the grime, you could see that the trousers must have once been brightly-striped.

"Kiss you, lady?" called the pirate captain, "Why you've a moustache as hairy as Blackbeard's!"

The old woman cackled with laughter. "Good luck to you, Calico Jack," she cried.

John Rackam was known as Calico Jack on account of his striped trousers. He was something of a ladies' man and known to have a softer heart than the average pirate. This was probably why his career as a pirate lasted for such a short time. But women loved him.

But it wasn't even Calico Jack who was attracting the crowds that day. The inhabitants of Spanish Town were accustomed to pirates and their trials, and executions no longer caused much of a stir. What drew them to the prison was the story going around that among the defendants this day were two women.

"It can't be true. It's impossible!" said one man, a pardoned ex-pirate himself. "No ship can take women – it's against the pirate rules, everyone knows that. It's punishable by death to smuggle a women on board – death for both parties."

The crowd strained forward as the defendants slowly emerged from the prison doors in a long line, blinking in the harsh glare of the sun. Two of them seemed slightly smaller than the others; they kept their heads down, shuffling along meekly in the group. But those who got a closer look could see that the two figures were curiously smooth-skinned. One of them looked up and grinned at the crowd. Her teeth were black pegs, her hair was covered by a dirty bandana and her face was black with grime - but she was recognizably a woman.

"It's Anne Bonny," cried someone, at which the woman shouted out defiantly.

"Yes, it's Anne Bonny. Have a good look before you see my petticoats swinging on a gibbet!"

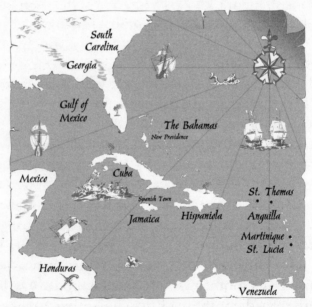

Map of the Caribbean, showing Spanish Town, Jamaica, where Anny Bonny and Mary Read were tried

Anne Bonny and Mary Read appeared in the Admiralty Court in Spanish Town, Jamaica in

November 28, 1720. They were on trial, along with the rest of Calico Jack's pirate crew, for an array of felonies that included the capture of seven fishing boats off the coast of the island of Hispaniola.

The women stood impassively, Anne Bonny, the insolent one, picking her teeth as the judge read out the list of their crimes. The judge who had seen many pirate trials in his time at the bar, looked up wearily at this sorry group.

"We'll try the women separately," he announced.

Anne Bonny stopped picking her teeth. "I'll be tried with my man," she shouted out, and she tried to reach across and put her hand in Calico Jack's.

Bonny and Read were the only two women ever known to have been allowed on a pirates' ship. They had come from vastly different backgrounds and yet they both longed for the freedom that came from living and working like a man.

Mary Read, the quieter of the two, had always lived like a boy. Born in England, she was the daughter of a woman whose husband had gone to sea and never returned. The woman already had one child by her husband – a son. But after he had left, she gave birth to Mary, whose father was another man. Mary's mother was desperately poor. When her young son died, she had no choice but to beg her mother-in-law for money. As the old woman knew nothing of this illegitimate daughter, Mary's mother dressed her up as a boy in order to pass her off as her dead son. She took Mary, in breeches and jacket, up to London, where the grandmother agreed to pay a crown a week for her upkeep.

So Mary spent her childhood dressed as a boy. Eventually, her mother found her a job as a young footman to a wealthy French woman who liked the young man's soft skin and pretty feaures. But Mary longed for adventure. Wearing gold brocade and serving soup out of tureens bored her. So, packing up her few possessions, she left for Flanders (now part of Belgium) and enlisted as a cadet in the army there. Remarkably, she managed to pass undetected as a soldier – and even distinguished herself by her courage on the battlefield, loading cannons and fighting in hand-to-hand combat with the enemy.

Mary shared a tent with a young Flemish soldier and told him of her identity. The two fell in love, left the army together and got married. They settled near the town of Breda in Holland where they set up as proprieters of a pub named the *Three Horse Shoes*. Then Mary's husband died, trade fell off, and Mary had to leave to seek her fortune elsewhere. So she dressed up as a man again and got a place on a ship to the West Indies. When the ship was captured by pirates, she joined them, still playing the part of a young man. Finally, she ended up on Captain Jack Rackam's ship – where she met Anne Bonny.

Anne had also been brought up as a boy – at least for a part of her childhood. She was the illegitimate "son" of a lawyer from County Cork and his household maid Peg Brennan. When the lawyer's jealous wife had Peg sent to prison for stealing silver spoons, Bonny's father had brought the bastard child to live with him, dressed up as a boy. He told everyone that she was a young man training as a lawyer's clerk. When his wife eventually discovered Anne's identity, there was a shocking scandal. The lawyer left hastily for America, taking Anne and her mother with him. They sailed to the Carolinas where he became a wealthy merchant and plantation owner.

Anne's father had high hopes for her. He wanted her to marry a rich man and settle down to the life of a leisured southern lady. But Anne was having none of it. Instead, she spent all the time she could down at the docks, talking to the sailors and trying to bribe herself a passage on a schooner. She fell in love with a poor sailor named Bonny, an unsuccessful former pirate and a drunk. When her father turned her out of the house, Anne married Bonny and they sailed to the island of New Providence, a notorious haven for pirates.

While every day her husband grew tipsier on the wharfside, Anne got to know the pirates who were lounging in the sun, tarring their ships, drinking, and waiting for the next big expedition. One of them singled her out. He was a slightly-built man with an engaging grin and distinctive striped calico trousers. It was John Rackam – otherwise known as Calico Jack. James Bonny seemed nothing but a weakling in comparison to Calico Jack. Jack gave her treasures – taken from a women's jewel case on a schooner off Jamaica. He flattered her, told her she was beautiful, and bowed elaborately when he saw her walking across the quay. Calico Jack was a charmer and Anne couldn't resist him. In a matter of months, she had left James Bonny sleeping off his rum and run away to sea with Calico Jack. She was dressed as a man to escape detection from the rest of his crew.

Anne was dropped off in Cuba to give birth to her first child, but Calico Jack soon sent for her again to rejoin his crew. It now had a new member: a soft-skinned young Englishman who spoke fluent Dutch. The legend goes that Anne thought the young man beautiful, and fell in love with him. What we do know is that she planned to reveal herself as a woman to entice the strange new pirate. But, when she did so, she got the surprise of her life: for the Dutch-speaking young man turned out to be Mary Read.

Back in Spanish Town, the judge had made his decision and the women were taken back to their cell. The men would be tried in a batch and the women would come to court after the others had been sentenced. Every man knew what that sentence would be – there was very little chance of getting off these charges.

For one thing, there were too many witnesses for the prosecution. The first one up in the dock was Thomas Spenlow, who described how the pirates had brazenly boarded his schooner and stolen fifty rolls of tobacco and nine bags of red Spanish peppers from the hold. They had tied him up and held him captive for about forty-eight hours – or so he said.

The pirates stared straight ahead. None of them had ever expected to have a long career in piracy, but all had once hoped that they might have been among the lucky ones, those who got out while they could, settling down to a God-fearing, law-abiding life, with the gold they had saved from thieving. But it was not to be. Calico Jack and his men knew from long experience that in a matter of days their bodies would be hanging from Gallows Point, a bleak and windswept promontory just visible through the bars of the court window.

And they were right. They were all found guilty and five of them were hanged by the neck the very next day. The broken body of Calico Jack, the wooing dandy, adored by the ladies, was screwed into an iron cage and swung from a gibbet on Deadman's Cay, where the seagulls pecked at his dead eyes.

When the gibbets were free again, it was time to bring Anne Bonny and Mary Read to trial. The two women had watched as their lovers were dragged from the prison to their deaths. Now they too had to await the certain verdict of the judge.

The evidence against them was as strong as it had been for the men. Two Frenchmen, who had been on board Spenlow's schooner when it was attacked, testified that Anne and Mary wore female clothes around the ship but changed into men's clothes at the prospect of an attack. The women did not shrink, they said, from carrying out the same violent work as the men. Thomas Dillon, master of the *Mary*, one of the sloops, described Anne Bonny with a gun in her hand, cursing and swearing.

Anne, with her black peg teeth, grinned from the dock, while Mary looked sullenly down at her boots. The judge, whose wife was a delicate lady who stayed indoors because of the heat, and who himself suffered from nervous headaches, listened amazed as he heard how Anne had slipped aboard the sloop and held a pistol to the two watchmen, threatening to blow out their brains.

The Royal Navy men who had finally captured Calico Jack and his crew told the court how the women had raged like "hell-cats" when they were discovered, how they had hurled themselves at the naval men, flailing at them with knives and cutlasses.

That same year, the two women had been present at the storming of a merchantman off the coast of Jamaica. There was a woman passenger on board, a Mrs. Thomas, who witnessed the event. She came to the court and, looking straight into the eyes of the two pirates, identified them as the two women who had screamed and hurled abuse at her. They were the same bloodthirsty bullies who had threatened to have her murdered. Mrs. Thomas remembered that they had been wearing long pants and baggy shirts which covered their bodies. "But," she said, "by the largeness of their breasts, I believed them to be women."

The judge didn't like sentencing women to death. But neither he nor, it seemed, Anne Bonny or Mary Read, could offer a single reason why they shouldn't suffer the same fate as their comrades.

He pronounced the sentence of death with his

usual slow solemnity. "You shall be taken from this place … And God in his infinite mercy be merciful to both your souls."

Anne and Mary were impassive at first. Mary continued to look at the floor, while Anne gazed defiantly around her. Then they whispered together for a moment, before one of them spoke up.

"We plead our bellies, sir."

The judge was flabbergasted. The women were pregnant. It was unthinkable that a court could hang a woman who was carrying a child.

The pair, grinning in triumph, were taken away to be examined by a local doctor who pronounced that it was true: they were both expecting babies. Their sentences of death were reprieved. But they both remained in prison. Mary Read contracted a fever and died a year later, but no one knows what happened to Anne Bonny – and she was still only 20 years old at the time she was sentenced.

Marooned

Of the thousands of islands that make up the Bahamas, few are habitable. Most of them consist of little but scorched coral reefs and dense scrubby interiors. They have no source of fresh water and no protection from the relentless rays of the sun which, reflected off a glassy sea, can drive a person heat-crazy in days. Nowadays the islands of the Bahamas are covered with hotels and marinas. People gather there to swim, scuba dive, play golf and eat lobster. But these islands were once the home only to pirates and their marooned victims.

Map of the Caribbean, showing New Providence, the pirates' haven

Marooning was the punishment that even the most hardened sailors feared more than any other. What more terrible, long-drawn-out death could be imagined than being abandoned to die on a waterless strip of rock, in the middle of a shark-infested ocean?

The victims were usually given a pistol. This was an act of mercy: there was nothing they could shoot for food. But they would need a bullet to take their own lives - although in the 17th century even a pirate believed he risked everlasting damnation in the fires of hell if he committed suicide. But that prospect might have seemed preferable to the long-drawn-out agony of dying parched and alone on a blazing rock.

Few survived a marooning, but those who did emerged as heroes. One of these was Captain William Greenaway. With seven of his fellow sailors, he was marooned on the desolate Bahamian island of Green Key. It was the penalty for their refusal to join the rest of their ship's crew who had mutinied in order to become pirates. Greenaway and his men were thrown stark naked onto the hot sands of Green Key, under a pitiless midday sun.

As they lay in the broiling hot sand, the men prepared themselves to die. There was no shelter and no water that they could see, except the rain that collected in hollowed-out stones, nothing but glimmering, salty, undrinkable water. The few trees were stunted and small, offering little protection from the sun. From the beach, they could see the sails of the pirate ship on the horizon. It appeared to pause momentarily on the rim of the sea then, shimmering as if it were a mirage, seemed to turn around. The men, watching through eyes that were already sore and dry from the heat, could scarcely believe their luck. It was coming back! They huddled together on the beach. Perhaps the pirates had relented, feeling they couldn't leave their former comrades to such a fate? Or perhaps they had decided that it would be kinder simply to kill them outright?

But it turned out that the pirates had no intention of picking up the men; they just wanted to compound their agony. They herded the naked sailors into a boat and rowed them out to a captured and now abandoned sloop which lay a mile offshore. They pushed the men into the sloop. But, instead of giving them a small chance to make a bid for freedom, they slashed the sloop's sails and rigging so that it had no chance of surviving even a day or two on the open ocean. Then they sailed away.

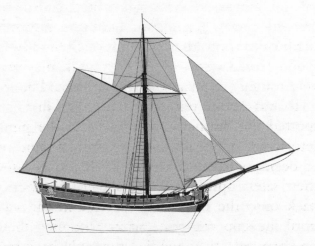

A 17th-century naval sloop

For the men on the sloop, matters looked even worse than they had done earlier. The ropes of the rigging dangled uselessly around them, and the tattered sails lay in ribbons all over the deck. The pirates had ensured that there was no food or water on board. The men would certainly have died on the boat had not one of them found a broken hatchet blade.

The captain saw immediately what could be done.

"I'll swim to shore," he said, and carefully tied the blade around his neck and leaped naked into the water.

It was a mile to the island but the water was sheltered and he managed it quite easily. Once he arrived, Greenaway used the blade to chop down trees and build rafts made from pieces of wood loosely tied with strips of sailcloth. These he paddled with his hands, over to the sloop, along with a small pile of berries cabbage palms and fruit. The men formed a relay, going backwards and forwards from the boat to the island, returning each time laden with wood. In this way, over the next week, they managed, very roughly, to repair the sails and mend the rigging.

It was about ten days later that their lookout spotted the distinctive silhouette of the pirate ship returning once again. The men held a rapid meeting to decide what they would do. It looked as though their safest option was to take to the rafts, paddle back onto the island, and lie low in the scrubland until the ship was gone again. Flattening themselves on their rafts, they paddled furiously back to Green

Key and hid, aghast, as they watched the pirates chop down the mast of the sloop and sink it in the open ocean. Then the ship sailed off again.

For the next week, the castaways gathered bitter berries (risking the possibility that they might be poisonous), and speared shellfish and sting rays with sharpened sticks. They also found a small spring, a source of brackish, but fresh, water. Meanwhile, the pirate ship circled the island like a shark. Sometimes they heard their former comrades calling out their names – but none of the men answered. They knew by now that the pirates only wanted them dead. They stood a better chance of staying alive by eating sour berries on a deserted island than by going back on board that ship.

The island was not as desolate as it had first seemed: the sailors found that with a little ingenuity it should be possible to survive for some time. They built themselves a makeshift shelter out of palms, which they leaned together in a teepee shape and bound together with coconut matting. At night they listened to the snuffling of wild hogs in the undergrowth. Bristly, spiny and brutish, these hogs were the main source of meat in the Caribbean, but they were vicious and strong and you couldn't catch them with your bare hands.

The men were growing desperate when the pirates returned yet again, sending an emissary onto the island with a promise that all was forgiven. After heated debate, they finally decided to trust the pirates. Hadn't they returned three times, after all? They must be feeling guilty. Perhaps they didn't want the lingering deaths of their former friends on their consciences? So the men emerged from the interior of Green Key and hailed the pirates from the beach.

But it turned out to be a terrible mistake. The pirates came ashore and made a show of welcome. But then they dragged Greenaway and two of his men to the ship, at the point of a musket, leaving the other five alone to meet their deaths on the island.

There the men remained for two more weeks, gathering what miserly scraps of nourishment the island had to offer. Then the pirates, returned yet again. Greenaway had argued hard with them, and eventually persuaded them to show a little mercy to the stranded sailors. So the pirates sent over a rowing boat containing a large cask of flour, a bushel of salt, 12 knives, some pots and pans, two guns and a store of gunpowder.

The castaways were still alone, but at least they could now use the guns to shoot hogs. They salted some of the meat (to preserve it) and ate the rest, roasted over a fire made by reflecting the sun off a gleaming knife blade. Then they built themselves a hut out of driftwood and rope that had been washed up on the shoreline.

For several weeks they waited, until again they spotted sails on the horizon. But, to their horror, it was only the pirate ship returning yet again. Whether out of guilt or sadism, the pirates seemed to be playing with the castaways. A posse of pirates swaggered ashore, ate their roast pork and burned down their hut.

But, in a gesture that the men now wearily recognized as typical, they left behind them a keg of rum, saying they would be back soon. The men uncorked the rum and each took a long swig. Then they sat on the hot white sand and contemplated their future. It had become clear to them that the pirates did not actually intend to kill them – but they were playing with them, as a cat plays with a mouse.

But the pirates never returned, because this time it was they who were the victims. Soon after they left the island for the open ocean, they were captured by a Spanish ship on the lookout for pirates. Captain Greenaway immediately told their captors the story of the castaways on Green Key and a boat was dispatched under the command of one John Sims. He drew his small boat ashore to find not a soul stirring on Green Key – and no sign of human habitation. The men were hiding up trees for fear that he was a pirate – or, even worse, their very own oppressors. Sims threw his musket to the ground and raised his arms to show that he was unarmed.

"Comfortable news," he shouted.

One by one, the men swung down from their trees, emaciated, bearded and dressed in tattered pieces of sailcloth.

Squinting in the sun, they gazed at Sims, and his ship, moored just beyond the edge of the lagoon.

They were so accustomed to the pirates' cruel pranks that they could hardly believe that this latest visitor was a friend. Then one of them slowly stepped forward across the sand. He extended his hand to Sims and, in a voice croaky with sun and salt, he finally spoke.

"Welcome sir, we are more than happy to see you."

A Spanish Novelist Escapes the Corsairs

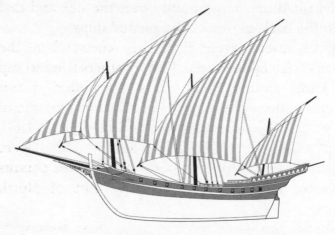

A galley used by Mediterranean pirates, known as corsairs

In 1575, two Spanish brothers, Miguel and Roderigo Cervantes, were sailing from the port of Naples, in the south of Italy, back home to Spain. They had been away for a long time, nearly three years, fighting in wars all over Europe. Miguel had had his hand cut off in battle. Both brothers were war-weary and looking forward to the end of their adventures.

When the corsair galleys attacked, the passengers hardly heard a thing. No sooner had the brothers woken to the sound of loud voices on deck but hands were clapped firmly over their mouths and they were dragged out of their hammocks. They bit and took swipes at their attackers, but it was no use. Several corsair vessels had drawn up alongside the ship and the brothers could see that it was pointless to resist. Along with several other passengers, they were loaded unceremoniously over the side and tied up in the back of one of the pirates' ships.

It was several days before they knew where the corsairs were taking them. Both brothers tried to slip the knots around their wrists, but found it too difficult to do without attracting the notice of one of the pirates. When at last they caught sight of land, they were unsure which country they were approaching – until they heard one of the corsairs announce it was Algeria, on the coast of North Africa.

Miguel and Roderigo and their fellow passengers were bundled out of the ship, their wrists still tied, and met on the beach by a man who handed over a bag of gold to the corsair captain, an Albanian named Arnaut Memi. Then they were made to walk for several hours, until they reached the city of Algiers. There, in a maze of narrow alleyways, they found themselves lined up in a market place, ropes around their necks, for sale as slaves. After what seemed like hours of haggling in a language none of them understood, Miguel was sold to an elderly Greek who took him home, loaded with iron chains.

Miguel was determined to be free, and continually concocted plans for escape. For two years his

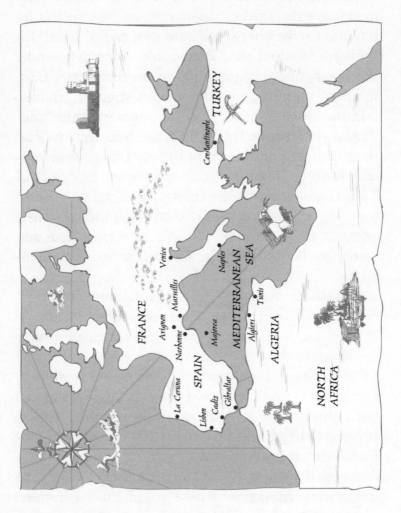

Map of the Mediterranean, the home of the corsairs

attempts failed and the watch over him grew stricter.

His brother Roderigo was luckier. He had been freed, after their father paid a ransom for him, but he refused to return home until he had secured his brother's freedom too. So he took up residence near the home of Miguel's employer. In secret meetings, the two brothers plotted, not only Miguel's getaway, but the return home of over 50 other Spaniards who had been kidnapped by corsairs and sold as slaves. The men had escaped their captors in a daring breakout, and Miguel had found them hiding, starving and terrified, in a cave. He secretly brought them food when he was allowed out of the house, and conspired with Roderigo to arrange a ship to rescue them and take them home. The ship was already on the horizon when their plan was discovered. The alarm was raised and the slaves were herded back into captivity.

Miguel took the blame for the failed escape on himself, and was taken in iron shackles to the palace of Hassan, the Viceroy of Algiers. There he was locked in a dungeon and tortured, but still he refused to implicate any of his fellow slaves in the plot. Hassan, who watched his suffering from the shadows, was so impressed by his courage that he persuaded the old Greek to sell him to him.

Miguel worked in Hassan's household for five desperate years, during which time he never stopped plotting to escape. He was on the point of being forced to go with Hassan to Constantinople (now Istanbul), in Turkey, when an elderly Spanish priest named Father Juan Gil came to visit the Viceroy.

Miguel watched him enter sullenly. He had given up on help from his fellow Spaniards. There had been no word from his father, no offers of assistance. All he knew now was that he would never give up trying to escape – however long it took.

But he didn't have to wait long. Father Juan Gil had brought with him a substantial ransom payment from Spain – a large enough sum of money even to satisfy Hassan. And so Miguel was released to return home. Later Miguel Cervantes became Spain's greatest novelist, the author of *Don Quixote*, putting to good use as stories his own extraordinary adventures.

The Conquest of the Quakers

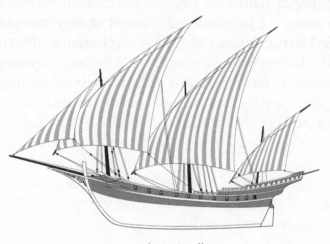

A corsair galley

It was late summer in 1663 and a ship was at anchor in the Thames at Greenwich, near London. It was an undistinguished ketch of the kind that could be seen on the river every day, and it bobbed gently on the water, its sails furled.

Over on Greenwich quay, a crowd of onlookers trained their eyes on the ketch, waiting for someone to come up from below decks.

"That's one of them," shouted a man suddenly, as a figure in sober black clothes appeared on deck. The crowd strained forward as a small rowing boat was lowered from the side of the ketch and began to move slowly towards the shore.

"Which one is it?" they whispered to each other as the boat came closer.

Just then there was a shout of, "Get out the way, folks. Make way for the King! Make way for the King!" and the people dispersed hastily.

A sedan chair carried by four sweating, panting footmen drew up at a spot with a grandstand view of the river. The crowd parted with a lot of curtseying and bowing, and a figure with heavy, sensual features and a small moustache climbed out of the chair. It was King Charles II, dressed in the finest silk and velvet and wearing a long, greasy black wig. He was followed shortly by another chair, this one carrying his brother, the Duke of York. The two men directed their gaze with the crowd towards the oncoming boat and laughed together.

"I wouldn't miss this story," said the King. "Would you believe it – the sailors who defeated the roughest Turkish corsairs with kindness!"

"It's scarcely believable," agreed the Duke, "and apparently they didn't even raise a single weapon to defend themselves!"

"Well, they didn't even have any weapons on board their ship – they don't believe in them."

"God obviously looks after Quakers!"

The rowing boat had pulled to shore by now and several men, most of them simply dressed in black, with no adornment, got out, roped it securely to an iron ring in the river wall and climbed the steps on to the quayside. When they saw the King, they didn't bow but simply nodded in respect. To the Quakers, everyone was equal, to be addressed only as brother or sister, no matter how grand or important they were.

"Which one of you is Thomas Lurting?" asked the King.

A man stepped forward. "I'm Thomas Lurting – first mate of this ship's company."

"Welcome, Mr. Lurting, now tell us your story," said the King.

The astonishing account of how Lurting and his fellow Quakers had escaped their pirate captors had made them heroes in London. For not only had they turned the tables on the pirates without raising a single hand in violence, but they had actually parted on good terms with them, swearing brotherhood at the end.

The Quakers had been the crew of a ketch bound from Venice on their return journey to England. In accordance with their religious beliefs, they carried no weapons on board – even though the Mediterranean at that time was teeming with pirates. The crew, who had heard reports that North African corsairs were particularly active in the area, had tried to persuade their captain to wait until they could arrange a convoy to accompany and protect their ship. Without weapons, they knew they wouldn't be able to put up any resistance if they were captured.

But the captain refused. Time was money and

waiting for a convoy would cost the owners of the ketch, as well as the tradesmen waiting for their goods from Venice. He decided he would take the risk and sail alone.

For the first few days, it looked as though the captain's gamble might have paid off. But, as they rounded the coast of Majorca, the island in the Spanish Balearics which the English used to call May-York, the men's hearts sank into their boots. On the horizon they could see a vessel moving at great speed – and it was heading straight towards them.

The strange ship, which they guessed from its flag was from Algeria in North Africa, chased them for several hours. But they couldn't escape. As the vessel finally drew alongside, the crew watched terrified as eight men jumped onto the side of the ketch, like agile spiders, and began to haul themselves up the ropes. They were heavily armed, with cutlasses in their belts and, in true pirate fashion, they had knives between their teeth.

In the account that Lurting later wrote of the incident, he remembered how terrified he was when he saw the Algerian pirates swarming up the sides of the ship. As all sailors knew, Algerian corsairs often sold their captives into slavery in North Africa – if they didn't kill them on the spot. But Lurting later described how he heard the words of the Lord run through him as he watched: "Be not afraid for all this, thou shalt not go to Algiers."

The words comforted him, and Lurting felt courage surging through him. Instead of cowering in fear from the attackers, he led the men in, greeting them warmly and welcoming them as friends.

At first the corsairs looked amazed. They surrounded the crew, their hands warily on their weapons, fearing that this odd reception must be some kind of trick. Then Lurting gestured that he wished to show them around the ship – as a hospitable host might show his guests around his home. As the corsairs walked around, opening the hold while Lurting explained to them about the details of the cargo, he reassured the rest of the crew in an undertone. He warned them to be very polite to the corsairs and added that he felt sure that he could find a way for them to escape their captors.

When the corsairs had recovered from their surprise at such a welcoming reception, and when they had reassured themselves that there were no arms on board, they decided they could relax. They retired to the captain's cabin to sleep off their exertions and, lulled into a false sense of security, instructed this odd English crew to point the ketch in the direction of Algiers and to sail it there.

Lurting then summoned his men and explained his plan. It should be easy, he reckoned, to overcome the invaders. After all, even though the crew had no weapons, they substantially outnumbered the corsairs. Now that the Algerians were all gathered downstairs in one part of the ship, they should be able to lash them together and sieze the ship back again. According to Lurting, one of the sailors was so fired up at the thought of the plot that he actually suggested that he might kill one or two.

Another joined him saying, "I would cut as many throats as you will have me."

But Lurting was horrified. He reprimanded the men sternly, reminding them that they were Quakers and bound not to kill anyone – even a common pirate. If he heard another word about killing or cutting throats, he threatened he would go straight below decks and tell the corsairs of their plan.

In the end, it proved astonishingly easy. The corsairs were snoring heavily in the cabin and it only took four men, creeping quietly down the hatch, to relieve them of their weapons and tie them together. They woke up to find themselves tied up and locked up by those oddly courteous gentlemen who had greeted them so politely when they first attacked them.

Now the Quakers were masters of their ship again. But they were faced with the problem of what to do with their captives. The obvious solution would have been to take them ashore at Majorca and leave them there. But Lurting pointed out that this would be an unchristian course of action, as the men would certainly be taken prisoner by the Spanish and forced to become slaves.

So he suggested that the pirates be returned safely to their own land. This was not as easy as it seemed. In fact, it was a rather dangerous proposition. If the Quakers anchored off Algeria, they themselves would certainly be taken into slavery. Any of the Quakers seen rowing the captives to shore would be seized immediately. So they argued and prayed about how it could be done, until at last the indomitable Lurting came up with another plan.

He seated all the corsairs in the small rowing boat, with the corsair captain in the stern and the others sitting next to each other, some on each others' laps. Then in climbed two Quaker sailors with an oar each. A third sat in the bows with a carpenter's axe (only to appear threatening – with no intention of ever using it, of course). Finally, Lurting got in and took the tiller. Under his legs he piled all the corsairs' weapons.

It took them more than two hours to pull to shore and the sailors panicked many times – sometimes claiming they saw heads waiting behind the rocks. But, finally, the boat scraped the sandy bottom of the shoreline and the pirates were hastily unloaded. When they were all on the beach, the Quakers threw them a large sack of bread and returned all their weapons. Amazed yet again by such treatment, the corsairs invited the men to stay, offering to take them to a nearby village where they could have a cup of wine together. Lurting thought it wise not to accept the offer. But he wrote later that, "we parted in great love, and stayed until they got up the hill, and then they shook their caps at us and we at them."

Back on board ship, the Quakers had a good wind and made it back to England without further incident. But no one spreads a good story as quickly as a sailor, and the tale of the Quakers' extraordinary escape by kindness was soon the talk of all the taverns where the ketch stopped over on the journey home. By the time Lurting and his fellows returned to London, they were heroes. Not that Lurting had much time for adulation. He was a simple man, with a simple, religious faith. He had no truck with monarchs and prestige and medals.

"Lurting, people talk of you of as a hero," said King Charles, as they stood on the quay at Greenwich under the bright September sun.

"It means nothing to me," replied the Quaker sailor. "I was doing only my duty."

And he meant it.

The Saint who Survived Slavery

In 1605, a young French priest named Father Vincent de Paul was making a sea voyage between the cities of Marseilles and Narbonne, on the south coast of France. The ship had the wind behind her and was moving at a steady pace. But, about halfway into their journey, as they were coasting along the Gulf of Lyons, the ship was attacked by three light, fast-moving Turkish sloops.

The corsairs pounced so quickly that three of the ship's passengers were killed, and many members of the crew were wounded, before they had even realized they were under attack. Vincent himself was hit by an arrow in his neck. It missed his artery, but he was bleeding heavily as he staggered on deck to see what was happening.

The corsairs poured on board, slashing to the left and right with knives and swords. Vincent later described them as being fiercer than tigers. He reported how, in revenge for the death of one of their men, they hacked one member of the ship's crew into a thousand pieces. The passengers and sailors were terrified. But the corsairs seemed content for a while to remain on the captured ship and made their prisoners stay in the cabins below while they ransacked the hold.

After about a week, the corsairs turned the ship away from France and set sail towards North Africa. When they arrived there, the prisoners were put up for sale as slaves in the city of Tunis and paraded five or six times through the streets with chains around their necks. The slavers' customers manhandled them roughly, inspecting them to see that they were fit and healthy and had not been injured when they were taken prisoner.

It was a fisherman who purchased Vincent. He kept him for a short period, and put him to work mending nets, before he sold him on for a tidy profit to an elderly alchemist – a follower of alchemy, the search for the legendary "philosophers' stone" that would make it possible to transform ordinary metals into gold. Here Vincent found a surprising friend. He described his new owner as a man of great gentleness and humility, and he found his work interesting too. Vincent's job was to stoke up the fires of ten or twelve huge ovens which the alchemist used for his experiments.

Vincent stayed with the alchemist for a year, until the old man died. Then he was sold on to a French outlaw who had taken refuge in the Tunisian mountains. Vincent so impressed him with his singing of the psalms that the outlaw's wife persuaded him to make his peace with the authorities back home in Avignon and release his slaves.

Vincent slowly made his way back to France. He walked most of the way, sleeping in the open air and begging food from villagers he met along the way. His long imprisonment had given him a sense of purpose: once he been a poor, desperate, ulcerated slave, and now he knew that all he wanted to do was to help other slaves.

Over the next forty years, Vincent worked tirelessly to establish hospitals for orphans and destitute women, and he founded a religious order devoted to nursing and helping the poor. He also helped the prisoners who worked in the galleys of the French king, remembering himself what it was like to be manacled in leg-irons and beaten. And he raised huge amounts of money to pay the ransoms of people who had been captured by corsairs and sold into slavery in North Africa. Nearly 1,500 slaves were freed as a result of his efforts. In 1727, seventy years after his death, Vincent de Paul was made a saint.

Mrs. Ching, the Terror of the South China Seas

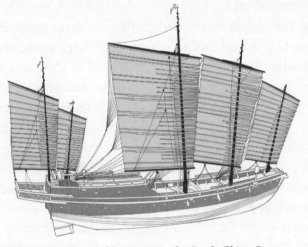

A Chinese junk, sailed by pirates in the South China Seas

The South China Seas have been swarming with pirates for centuries. Two hundred years after pirates had been almost completely wiped out in the Caribbean, and in the Indian Ocean, ships in the South China Sea were still regularly being attacked by formidable fleets of sailing ships known as junks.

European pirates would never have dared to threaten the monopoly of the Chinese pirate empires, which ran expeditions of terror and robbery all the way down the South China coast. These waterborne armies sometimes numbered hundreds of vessels. And there was little any merchant ship could do to stand against them.

In 1809, Richard Glasspoole was an officer serving in the East India Company, when he was attacked and captured by pirates in the South China Sea. He and some fellow officers had been returning to their ship, the *Marquis of Ely*, after spending some days on the island of Macau.

The men were covering the few miles between Macau and the ship in an open boat, when a sudden fog made navigation impossible. In the thick, wet gloom, they couldn't even see their hands in front of their faces. By the time the fog had lifted, several hours later, Glasspoole and his companions had floated far off course.

For several days, drifting without food or water in the middle of the open ocean in their tiny boat, the men had resigned themselves to a slow death. When the distinctive, fin-like sails of a small fleet of junks appeared in the distance, they were amazed to see signs of life. They stood up in excitement, waving their arms to attract attention.

But they could not have known that the junks belonged to Chinese pirates, known as ladrones? As one of the junks, which they assumed was just a fishing vessel, drew alongside, they were taken by surprise when twenty ladrones leaped up from their hiding place at the bottom of the boat. The pirates pulled their short, sharp swords against the mens' necks then looked at their officer for his orders. The terrified Englishmen watched as he ceremoniously sheathed his sword – the signal not to kill them.

Instead the pirates dragged the men on board the junk and chained them to the deck. Glasspoole, who could speak some Cantonese, entered into a long negotiation with the pirates about what they could ask for a ransom. Finally, it was decided to write to the English authorities in Macau, demanding 70,000 dollars in exchange for their lives. A boat was sent off with the message.

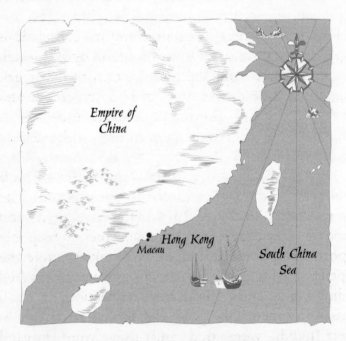

Map showing the South China Sea, where Chinese pirates sailed in fleets of ships called junks

Meanwhile, the captives lay and waited. They were chained together on the deck of the junk, and given nothing to eat or drink. After several days, they saw an extraordinary, frightening, sight: the approaching sails of at least 500 junks. At first the men dared to hope that it might be a squadron of the Chinese navy, and that rescue might be near at hand. But it turned out to be the rest of the pirates' fleet, joining their fellows for some pillaging of the towns and villages along the coast and even far up the rivers. It was highly organized – each junk flying a flag of a different type – indicating which squadron it belonged to.

For several weeks, Glasspoole and his companions were kept in chains and forced to stand by and watch as the ladrones extracted money from the villagers. The junks would anchor outside a settlement and threaten to burn down the village and rob its inhabitants if they did not receive a handsome payment.

They were as good as their word. If the villagers could not afford the so-called contribution, the pirates would move in, destroying rice fields and hacking down groves of orange trees. Glasspoole reported that some fisherman were taken before the captain of his junk, when they were discovered hiding up a creek, with their collection of small boats. Sickened, Glasspole was forced to watch as their hands were tied and they were hoisted screaming above the deck – for refusing to take the oaths that would bind them in the service of the ladrones forever. The fishermen were brutally flogged until they seemed to be dead and then left hanging from the mast until they were actually dead, or had pleaded to take the oath of allegiance to the pirates.

It seemed as though the Englishmen's ordeal would never end. They wondered if the ladrones' ransom letter had ever reached English officials in Macau. Did anyone actually know that they were still alive? They never even left the junks. It seemed that the ladrones had no homes on land, but lived with their wives and families in cramped quarters aboard their junks. Rats swarmed everywhere – they were regarded as a great delicacy, particularly baby ones, and encouraged by the pirates to breed. The river water was sluggish and brown and mosquitoes circled everywhere in thick swarms, causing constant itching and scratching. Glasspoole and his friends spent three weeks eating nothing but boiled rice cooked with caterpillars. At night, they watched the pirates light up their opium pipes and play cards until dawn.

It was two or three weeks into their captivity that one of the pirates told Glasspoole and his friends that the "admiral" wished to meet them.

"The admiral is very strict," said the pirate, "and a great fighter." Glasspoole was wary but intrigued.

The flagship turned out to be a large and spacious junk, slightly less infested with vermin than the others. It flew a red flag, which signified the senior squadron. Glasspoole could see no one on board but two armed guards and a tiny middle-aged woman sitting on the deck. The pirate accompanying him bowed low towards the woman and Glasspole was astonished to see that this tough brute of a man looked almost afraid. The pirate whispered in Glasspole's direction,

"This is the admiral."

The Englishman was speechless – the leader of this massive fleet of five hundred marauding ships was a woman.

"I am Mrs. Ching," said the woman to Glasspoole, when he had recovered from his surprise.

He too bowed low in response. He had heard some stories of a pirate woman who ravaged the coast and rivers of China, but had dismissed the tales as too fantastic to believe.

Mrs. Ching treated Glasspoole politely. She told him that she always took care that her men's conduct was kept under strict control. Glasspoole did not dare say that he had not noticed any restraint among the pirates. But Mrs. Ching insisted that she liked to maintain standards.

"I have laid down laws," she told him. "For example, if any of my men goes ashore on his own to drink, he gets his ears perforated as a punishment. Furthermore, my pirates are entitled to exactly 2% of the value of the goods they take, and if any man takes any more he will be executed. And, what is more than that – if a pirate wishes to behave violently towards a woman in the village, he may only do so if he has permission from the purser first."

Glasspoole was appalled but fascinated by Mrs. Ching. She kept him on her junk for several hours, boasting about her organization, and how her pirate empire had successfully destroyed almost all its rivals. Clearly a clever businesswoman, she apparently considered herself a legitimate trader. She told him proudly that every single piece of plunder taken in their raids was entered precisely in a log book which she kept at a warehouse in a secret location.

"I don't like to use the word *plunder*," she told him. "I prefer to refer to my cargo as *trans-shipped goods*."

Mrs. Ching ordered that Glasspoole and his friends be given a berth on her flagship. She wanted them to witness her powers of leadership in action. They were horrified when she also demanded that they man guns on behalf of the pirates. When they objected, Mrs. Ching gave them a long, cold, look and suggested that they might rethink their objections under torture.

In the battles that followed, Glasspoole was twice nearly killed by cannon balls. He observed that the pirates had a custom of mixing gunpowder with their strong drink before a battle, as it gave them added courage. It also made their faces and eyes turn a boiling red - which terrified their enemies. During the thickest fighting, he was startled when Mrs. Ching approached him with a small silver bottle in her hand and sprinkled him with a pungent, oniony-smelling liquid.

"It's garlic water," he was told, "a charm to protect you against bullets."

In the course of their three months with the ladrones, the Englishmen learned more about Mrs. Ching and her life. She was the widow of a bloodthirsty pirate admiral, who had been murdered by the inhabitants of a coastal town which he had burned and destroyed. On her husband's death, Mrs. Ching had taken command of his fleets and, under her, they had become even more successful than ever. There was nothing the Chinese government could do to stop the pirates now – they were the most powerful force in the land.

The government of the Chinese Emperor Jiaqing had made attempts to crush the pirates before – but without success. It had once won a significant victory when a fleet of warships was sent to attack the pirates, and set fire to hundreds of light, wooden pirate junks. But even the loss of large numbers of her men and boats was not enough to deter Mrs. Ching. She gathered her forces, uniting with two other pirate chiefs to increase her manpower, and sailed off to find the government fleet. When they reached it, the sailors were caught off guard, relaxing after what they thought was their victory. That night, the pirates sprang their surprise attack, pouring over the decks with flaming brands and knifing anyone and burning anything that came in their way. The Emperor's fleet was almost completely destroyed; only 100 men survived.

Glasspoole and his friends had begun to lose all hope that they would ever return home. Then word suddenly came that their ransom had been paid in full. The pirates let them go, even escorting them up the river to the nearest port.

But Mrs. Ching continued to terrorize the Chinese shipping trade. Her pirate empire finally came to an end when the leader of her "black flag" squadron deserted her and surrendered to the Emperor. He took with him 8,000 men, 165 ships, 500 guns and 5,600 other weapons. In return, the government presented him with a pardon and two towns for his men and their families to settle in.

Mrs. Ching's position was now precarious. Many of her pirates looked at the privileges given to the Black Flag Squadron and thought they might enjoy them too. Even Mrs. Ching herself was tiring of a life of constant battle. After some negotiation with the government, it was agreed that she, and any of her men who gave themselves up, would be officially pardoned. On top of this, they would be presented with a large quantity of pork and wine and a sum of money. The pirate stranglehold was broken at last.

Not that Mrs. Ching settled down to a comfortable, stay-at-home life. She ended her days running a highly successful smuggling business.

The Black Joke

A US warship, used to guard against pirates in the the Caribbean

One hundred years after the death of Blackbeard, Bartholomew Roberts and Henry Every, pirates were becoming scarce. They had already become legends rather than real threats, tales to scare and fascinate children with, with stories of walking the plank, pieces of eight and buried treasure.

But the sailors who navigated the shipping channels of the world knew that piracy, athough it was rare, had not disappeared altogether. In the 1820s, the seas were swollen with new vessels carrying cargo further and further across the newly industrialized world. And, in 1820 alone, 27 American ships were attacked at sea.

Between 1821 and 1822, an American warship named *Enterprise*, commanded by Lieutenant Commander Lawrence Kearney, had captured four pirate schooners while patrolling the waters off the Gulf of Mexico. Their captain was a sleazy latterday pirate named Charles Gibbs. He was a murdering brute, who had chopped off the arms and legs of a captain he had taken hostage earlier in the year. On another occasion, he had burned an entire crew of merchant sailors to death.

If the cruelty of pirates was unabated – and in the case of Gibbs, it was entirely for his own horrible pleasure – the spoils of piracy were small compared to the glittering prizes that could have been won a century earlier. Once ships had carried gold, silver and silks between the world's most powerful monarchs – but now they transported coal, timber and fish oils for the new industries of Europe and America. One of the American warships stationed in the Caribbean reported in 1822 that the pirates who boarded his ship escaped with nothing more than a ship's compass, a pot of hot potatoes from the galley, sixteen dollars from the captain's trunk, some cooking pots and a ball of twine.

The pirates of the 19th century lacked the bravado and flamboyance of the pirates of the Golden Age. Where Bartholomew Roberts and Henry Every had displayed their skills of seamanship and leadership, these latterday pirates were merely opportunists and bandits, out to steal whatever they could find. And they were particularly nasty.

In the 1830s, a Portuguese pirate named Benito da Soto acquired a reputation among sailors for exceptional cruelty and savagery. In his ship, aptly named the *Black Joke*, da Soto was reputed to have blown the brains out of a man who had helped him steer the ship into a Spanish port, saying, "You have done well, my man, I'm obliged to you."

In 1832, a British ship, the *Morning Star*, was sailing home through the South Atlantic. As dawn rose, the terrified watch reported that the *Black Joke* was chasing them at some speed. Before the captain had time to act, the pirates had blasted the ship with cannon shot, shredding her rigging. The *Morning Star* was forced to surrender: many of the sailors were injured and the ship was taking in water fast and in danger of sinking.

Benito da Soto sent orders to the captain of the *Morning Star* that he must come over to the *Black Joke* immediately. The captain consulted with his officers. They all knew da Soto's reputation for mindless savagery. But the captain realized that he had little choice but to do what the pirate wanted. After all, he reasoned, he might be able to negotiate with them.

But it cost him his life. When he was standing before da Soto on the deck of the *Black Joke*, the pirate chief spat contemptuously in his face, then raised his cutlass. With a single blow, he brought it down on the captain's head, slicing it in two, right down to his jawbone.

The passengers and crew of the *Morning Star* waited anxiously for the captain's return. But it was da Soto and his men who appeared on the deck instead. They herded the crew together and looted what few goods they could find that had not already been destroyed by their gunfire. Then they threw everyone into the ship's hold, riddled the hull with gunshot and left.

It seemed certain that the ship would sink. By now it was listing dangerously in stormy seas, and water was pouring in. But the crew miraculously managed to force open a hatch, and worked the pumps. The *Morning Star* limped her way to Gibraltar, where da Soto was later recognized by some members of the crew. He was arrested, tried and hanged in Cadiz, in Spain.

Da Soto's reign of terror in the *Black Joke* had ended. It was the last time a pirate would wield such power over the trade routes of Europe and America.

Sir Henry Morgan, the King's Pirate

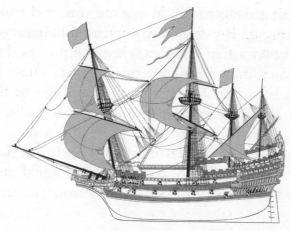

A 17th century galleon

In 2004, a team of divers off the coast of Haiti saw, in the clear aquamarine water, a barnacled iron cannon rolling gently in the surf. One of the divers swam in a little further. The waters in this isolated spot, near the offshore island of L'Ile de Vache, are just twelve feet deep. But they are also extremely dangerous. When the divers approached to get a closer look, they were pounded by forty foot waves, and pulled off course by treacherous currents.

But the moment they saw the cannon tumbling in

the breakers, the diving team knew that they had found what they had been looking for: the remains of Captain Henry Morgan's wrecked ship HMS *Oxford*. The *Oxford* had sunk in 1669, after an explosion which killed 350 members of her crew. The explosion was reportedly triggered by a spark from a pig roast on the deck, which ignited the gunpowder magazine and blew the front of the ship away. The swashbuckling Morgan was dining below deck in his luxurious cabin when the ship exploded, and he was thrown through a porthole.

By some miracle, Morgan managed to survive the buffeting of the waves and swim over to another vessel in his fleet – a captured French ship named *Le Cerf Volant*. And so he was able to return to his base in Jamaica. In 1675, he took command of a new ship, the *Jamaica Merchant*, and set out again for L'Ile de Vache, to try to salvage some of the looted Spanish treasure he had hidden in the *Oxford*. But the seas there were too powerful even for such an experienced sailor, and the ship went down in a hurricane.

Morgan survived again. But that was no surprise, as Morgan was a born survivor. By 1674, he had become Sir Henry Morgan, Deputy Governor of Jamaica, the wealthy ally of King Charles II, and the owner of a prosperous sugar plantation worked by hundreds of slaves.

But Morgan was also a pirate and one of the most successful at that. He disguised his activities under a commission from the British government, calling himself a "privateer" who only robbed from Spain because she was his country's enemy. But among the pirates of Jamaica he was known as "the pirate king" – and they knew full well that, under his fashionable clothes and periwig, Morgan was as ruthless, greedy and bloodthirsty as any of those pirates who ended their careers on the end of the hangman's rope.

Morgan was born in Monmouthshire, Wales, in 1635, the son of a poor farmer. As a boy, he was sent as a worker to Barbados. The Caribbean was a hotbed of pirates and the young Morgan quickly realized that a life of piracy would bring him far greater rewards than a life of toil. He joined a ship and his leadership skills soon won him a reputation as a good captain. Morgan was a sensualist; he liked the fine things of life – the best wine, delicious food, elegant clothes – and he had spotted the quickest route to winning them for himself. But he was clever enough to see that he could cover his back if he made a career in "legitimate" thieving. With a royal commission for plundering Spanish ships in his pocket, the government might even hail him as a hero who had filled British coffers with enemy gold.

In 1667, Britain and Spain had signed a treaty in Madrid, in which they promised not to attack each others' ships. But each country decided on a different interpretation of the treaty. The Spaniards assumed the West Indies and America were excluded, while the British assumed that they were included. It wasn't long before the pact broke down completely. Months later, Sir Thomas Modyford, the Governor of Jamaica, heard that Spaniards in Cuba were preparing a force to attack and sieze the British colony of Jamaica.

Modyford was thrown into panic. His military fortifications were inadequate and his only option was to call up a mercenary force made up of pirates. There was no money to pay them wages, so Modyford permitted them to keep any booty that they might find on the invading Spanish ships.

This was Henry Morgan's moment – and he grasped it. From now on, he would steal, plunder and torture as much as he wanted – and all with government permission. The colonial government in Jamaica granted him a special commission under which he could gather a motley army of pirates to invade Cuba. They were to take as many Spanish prisoners as was necessary to extract information about the forthcoming attack on Jamaica. And along the way, of course, they had permission to seize anything of value that they might find. Morgan assembled a small fleet of ships and sailed for Cuba.

After torturing several Spaniards that they imprisoned during their raid on the Cuban settlement of Puerto del Principe, Morgan's men were able to confirm that a Spanish attack was indeed planned on Jamaica. Morgan could congratulate himself that he had fulfilled his part of the contract, and he relayed the information to Modyford. But the loot in Puerto del Principe was disappointing and the pirates grew restless.

Morgan promised them that greater treasure would be found in the wealthy Spanish port of Puerto Bello, on the mainland of Central America. There were some Englishmen in prison in the town, and Morgan planned to rescue them – further proof of the law-abiding, patriotic motives of his campaign.

"It's our duty, men," he shouted, stirringly, at the shabby group of ruffians he had gathered on the ship's deck. "We are working for His Majesty King Charles against wicked Spaniards who are plotting to overthrow us."

The men rolled their eyes and grinned. They knew Morgan's game. He was as interested in his patriotic duty as they were. Like them, it was gold he really wanted – and lots of it.

Morgan's fleet anchored thirty miles off Puerto Bello. Through their telescopes, they could make out the three huge forts that defended the town. They were reputed to be impregnable. A surprise attack was the only solution, but it would be very dangerous. Using canoes, a force of 400 pirates paddled silently into the port by night. They launched a flash raid on the first fort, wielding knives and muskets, and slaughtering indiscriminately; 74 out of 130 Spanish soldiers were killed. Then they found the English prisoners and released them, before moving on to the second fort.

This fort was more heavily defended than the other two, and the pirates only succeeded in scaling its walls by using monks and nuns that they had captured in the town as living shields. The terrified captives screamed as they were pulled up the rope ladders by men whose hands were already sticky with blood. When they reached the third fort, its guards surrendered immediately.

The pirates had a one-month reign of terror over Puerto Bello. They pillaged the town, looted every building and tortured the townspeople, slitting off their ears and noses, until they revealed the hiding places of their treasures. By the time the pirates had left for home, they were carrying an impressive haul of gold, silver and jewels. In his account of the raid, Morgan laid great emphasis on how they had courageously rescued the English prisoners. He said nothing at all about any of their other activities.

If Modyford felt uneasy about Morgan's methods, he said nothing about it. Morgan and his men were popular national heroes in Jamaica, and with every new expedition that was launched under the auspices of their royal commission, the plunder that they brought back to the island boosted the economy. Morgan himself bought a large Jamaican estate and lived there in gentlemanly style, waited on by slaves.

In 1670, Morgan embarked on his most daring expedition yet: an attack on the Pacific port of Panama, the richest and most important Spanish city in Central America. He recruited 2,000 pirates to join him. Panama was heavily defended, and Morgan decided to approach via the River Chagres. In 36 river boats and canoes, a force of 300 pirates slid quietly through the dense, insect-infested jungle. It took them nine days. About three miles outside Panama, they found an army of 2,000 men waiting for them. Morgan and his men turned back, approached the city by another route and took it by surprise. Panama now belonged to the pirates.

The pirates rampaged over the city, looting, torturing and murdering. While they were in command, a fire swept through the narrow streets, reducing much of the city to embers. Morgan's men stole Spanish ships anchored in the port and sailed them triumphantly back to Jamaica, where they were given a heroes' welcome. The Governor himself publicly thanked them for crippling Spanish military and naval power.

But, back in Britain, the government was feeling uneasy about Henry Morgan's exploits. The country was on the brink of war with the Dutch, and wanted to make sure that Spain remained neutral. The attack and devastation wreaked on Panama was a serious embarrassment. In London, when the Spanish Ambassador furiously complained about Morgan and Modyford, government ministers nodded in agreement. They threw up their hands when they were told of the horrors perpetrated on Spanish colonists, and promised that they would do everything in their power to punish the evildoers.

So Modyford and Morgan were summoned home to England, "to answer for crimes against the King, his crown and dignity." Morgan spent three years in London waiting to hear what the King planned to do with him. Modyford was given a very comfortable room in the Tower of London, but Morgan was never even arrested. In fact, he was treated like a hero. Modyford staunchly defended him, claiming that Jamaica would now be in the hands of the Spanish were it not for Henry Morgan.

Eventually, both men were sent back to their estates in Jamaica, where Morgan was given the post of Deputy Governor and a knighthood. He was now Sir Henry Morgan, gentleman and patriotic hero. He died at home in his bed in 1688, at the age of 53. Due to the copious amounts of rum he drank every day, it was alcoholic poisoning that killed him in the end.

Also from Usborne True Stories

TRUE STORIES OF
SPIES

PAUL DOWSWELL & FERGUS FLEMING

"In all your years of fame," Kramer
explained delicately, "you have known
some of the most powerful men in
Europe. Would you consider returning to
Paris now to mingle again with these
influential gentlemen? And, while you're
doing this, might you be able to keep me
informed of anything interesting they
might say?"
Margaretha looked curious but
non-committal.
Kramer went on, "We could pay you well
for this information – say 24,000 francs."

What are real spies like? Some, like beautiful Mata
Hari, are every bit as glamorous as famous fictional
agents such as James Bond. But spies usually live
shadowy double lives, risking prison, torture and
execution for a chance to change history.

TRUE STORIES OF
ESCAPE

PAUL DOWSWELL

Finally, the night had come to take a
trip to the roof. Morris spent the day
beforehand trying to curb his restlessness.
What if the way up to the roof was
blocked? What if the ventilator motor
had been replaced after all? All their
painstaking work would be wasted. The
12 year sentence stretched out before
him. Then another awful thought
occurred. The holes in the wall would
be discovered eventually, and that would
mean even more years added on to
his sentence.

As well as locked doors, high walls and barbed
wire, many escaping prisoners also face savage dogs
and armed guards who shoot to kill. From Alcatraz
to Devil's Island, read the extraordinary tales of
people who risked their lives for their freedom.